GREEK DANCES FOR AMERICANS

GREEK DANCES
FOR AMERICANS

by Rozanna Mouzaki

Translated from the Greek by Athena G. Dallas-Damis

1981
DOUBLEDAY & COMPANY, INC., GARDEN CITY, NEW YORK

I would like to thank the Demoglou and Stratou dancers for agreeing to let me use their photographs in this book. I also acknowledge with grateful appreciation the photographer of these groups, Mr. Nikos Kontos.

Overleaf, Dance of Roumeli; page i, Harvest Dance of Cyprus (both photos of Dora Stratou Dancers); opposite, the Zorba dance.

DIAGRAMS BY ANDREAS TSOMBOS
BOOK DESIGN BY BEVERLEY VAWTER GALLEGOS

Library of Congress Cataloging in Publication Data
Mouzaki, Rozanna.
   Greek dances for Americans.
Includes index.
1. Folk dancing—Greece.   2. Folk dancing,
Greek—United States.   I. Title.
GV1653.M6813   793.3′19495
ISBN: 0-385-14041-X
Library of Congress Catalog Card Number 77–25604

Dedicated to what I have loved most in life

Contents

PREFACE   *ix*

INTRODUCTION   *x*

A BRIEF HISTORY OF GREEK DANCE   *1*

   The Ancient Greeks and Their Dances   *1*
   Modern Greeks and Their Dances   *5*
   The Anastenaria   *12*

GREEK DANCES TODAY   *16*

   Greek Costumes   *17*
   The Handkerchief in Traditional Folk Dances   *19*
   The Dances in This Book   *20*

TRADITIONAL FOLK DANCES   *22*

   Kalamatianos   *23*
   Syrtos   *40*
   Tsamikos   *55*

DEMOTIC OR TRADITIONAL MUSIC   *73*

   The Demotic or Traditional Folk Orchestra   *74*

POPULAR FOLK DANCES   77

   Hassapikos   78
   Hassaposervikos   105
   Syrtaki   113
   The Zorba   123
   Zeibekikos   135

POPULAR FOLK MUSIC   152

   The Popular Folk Orchestra   153

GREEK COSTUMES   155

   Women's Folk Costumes   155
   Men's Folk Costumes   160
   The Evzones   167

LET'S HAVE A GREEK PARTY   168

INDEX   172

Above, an ancient frieze showing a Pyrihios' dance.

Rozanna Mouzaki

Preface

My fear friends, welcome! Welcome to the exciting world of Greek dancing. Relax and forget your daily cares for a little while, as the people of Greece do. For the dance is their expression of joy and sadness, of exuberance and forgetfulness. Come with me, dear readers, and learn who I am and what I love most in life.

I am Rozanna Mouzaki. My name may ring a bell for many of you. I am the one who has been telling you for the past fifteen years, "Go Greek!" The phrase "Go Greek!" was born in my dance studio on Manhattan's Eighth Avenue. From there it accompanied me to larger quarters on Madison Avenue, and later to West 55th Street. Soon, "Go Greek!" was being heard all over New York and shouted at many events throughout the city—at the United Nations and municipal festivals, at the World's Fair, at Carnegie Hall, in New York *tavernas* and eateries. In time, my invitation, "Go Greek!" was spreading throughout the country.

As you turn the pages of this book you will hear it again, and a voice will be whispering, "Have fun the Greek way . . . come, all of you, and learn the Greek dances, whatever your ethnic background." For dancing knows no country or nationality—it is universal, all-encompassing. It is a silent language understood by everyone, everywhere.

It is in this language, the language of the dance, that I communicate with you now. This is not meant to be a literary work, for I am not a writer. I am merely someone who has devoted her life to serving the wonderful art of the dance, and who now wants to share it with you.

Greek Dances for Americans is my gift to the adopted land I have come to love as much as the land of my birth. Thank you for sharing your country with me so warmly, so affectionately. Now let me share a bit of my Greece with you!

Introduction

My story begins in the early 1940s during the German occupation of Greece, in Patras, a town in the Peloponnese in southwestern Greece.

I vaguely remember when I first realized I was completely alone in the world, not knowing where I came from or where I was going. Perhaps this confusion in my life was the reason I avoided people and enclosed myself in a circle of my own, a protective loneliness. In this haze of memories I remember an inner world filled with questions and confused feelings. It was during those puzzled moments of my childhood that I felt a strange, beautiful emotion. I was not yet five years old when I sensed the first flutterings of my heart at the sound of music—any kind of music. Soon my feet began to keep tempo with those flutterings. The tap-tap of the rhythm inside me became my first dance steps that were to develop into the full rhythmic movements of the professional dancer. What did I care that I had no family? I had the dance—I would soar!

My second vivid memory is the Zouroudi School of Ballet, one of the few ballet schools in Athens at that time. It was here that the great Athenian dancer-choreographer, Stavros Spiropoulos, saw me and took me on as a student. Through him I learned discipline, hard work, full devotion to my art. Soon I was a member of his dance group. The hours became days, the days years, slipping by quickly as my life completely evolved in dancing, in endless exercise. We toured Egypt, Casablanca, Cyprus, Turkey, Beirut. It was exciting, being a part of all this.

Then came the big surprise. Stavros Spiropoulos, the man who taught me to dance, selected me as his partner. A whole new world opened up for me. I was to begin gathering the fruit of my labor. The Spiropoulos group toured Europe and the Orient, with Spiropoulos and myself as the stars. My childhood dream was coming true.

But time takes its toll, and after thirty-four years of dancing the famous Spiropoulos felt it was time to give up public appearances and devote his talent exclusively to teaching. However, he felt an obligation toward the girl he had helped into the limelight, and was determined to help her continue

My first group of students going through their paces.

Here I am in my first New York studio, teaching the Hassapikos to three young dancers.

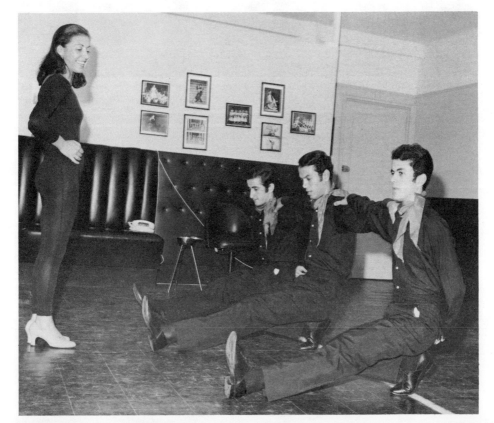

My troupe performed at many Greek affairs in the New York area.

Below, the Rozanna Mouzaki Dancers on stage at Town Hall.

her career. There was little opportunity for a lone dancer in Greece at the time, so he introduced me to the Dutch Dance Group of Joseph Baresci. I was overjoyed when Baresci took me on as leading female dancer of his group in Amsterdam.

At that time, Baresci was one of the leading choreographers of expressionistic dancing, and his group performed in all the European capitals. I was happier than I had ever been. What glorious moments—I can still hear the warm applause of those wonderful international audiences.

As time passed, a sadness came over me. I was lonely—of all the nationalities in our dance group, I was the only Greek, and I longed for the warmth of my own people. To be in my homeland and speak my language, to share the same customs with other people were desires that grew into a desperate need. When I could ignore it no longer, I decided to change my plans for the future. My first thought was to return to Greece. But I knew I had no family waiting for me there, no one to welcome me back. And then I thought of other Greeks living away from home. Would they, too, not feel the same nostalgia, the same loneliness? I would bring them my dancing, and perhaps they would welcome me into their circle. And so, sixteen years ago, I set out for the United States with a new goal—to be an artist in this great country I had heard so much about.

Soon after my arrival in New York, I was fortunate to meet the famous Greek troubadour, Nicos Gounaris. We sat for hours and talked about the Greek Americans, their way of life, their hopes, their ways of entertainment. He explained to me that Greek Americans love song and dance, in the spirit of their countrymen across the seas. In a short time I witnessed the truth of Nicos' words. And I was more determined than ever to offer the best I had in me, to share my great love for dancing with America. This would be my career here.

The Greek-American organizations welcomed me, first in New York and then in various cities throughout the country. I visited their schools and churches, observed their social and cultural lives, their programs, their fun and gaiety. I did not feel a stranger in this new land, for I was embraced as a member of the great Greek family in America. I developed my own act and performed frequently in New York and other cities. And I continued to study the American way of life the Greeks enjoyed while holding onto the traditions of their own heritage. I soon learned, however, that no organized group of Greek dancers existed in America. There was no one to present the beautiful dances of Greece at American universities, at the United Nations, and at the countless ethnic festivals held in cities throughout the country.

And so the idea for the creation of a Greek Dance Company in New York was born. In 1970, I took the first step toward fulfilling that dream by opening the first studio of Greek dance in New York. Just as I had imagined, people were anxious to learn Greek dancing. They came with enthusiasm and applied themselves with zeal. My studio took on an air of gaiety and warmth. The will and diligence of my first students would be my strength for the next step: the actual formation of a Greek dance company.

From the studio I selected the dancers for the company and began to work with them, putting all my knowledge and strength to the task ahead. To enrich the group, I added new members, taught them the dances, choreographed variations, designed and ordered costumes. The work was tedious and long, but I was encouraged by the continued enthusiasm of my pupils. The company was on its way.

Melina Mercouri, Jules Dassin, and I at the first-night party for the film Ilya Darling, *for which I choreographed the Greek dances.*

Governor Nelson Rockefeller at the New York World's Fair, 1964, congratulating me for my act and receiving in turn a Greek Evzone doll on behalf of the Greek people.

As word of my dance studio spread, friends and many others in New York and other cities expressed regret that they could not attend my classes in Greek dancing. They kept asking for some form of instructions and diagrams, perhaps a booklet that might help them learn Greek dancing. And so I began to think of putting together a small book that would bring my studio to those who could not come to it. In this I would teach anyone and everyone how to dance Greek, regardless of where they lived or what their ethnic background might be.

For my *Greek Dances for Americans* I selected the Greek dances that are most popular and most danceable in this country. To these I added instructions and simple diagrams. A short history accompanies each dance to give you a general picture of how it evolved, how the ancient Greeks used the dance as a means of expressing emotion, and how we feel about it today.

Statue of the goddess Athena from the Archaeological Museum in Athens.

A Brief History of Greek Dance

Dance is defined as a succession of body movements, rhythmic steps, and hand movements that follow a predetermined pattern and are performed to the sound of music.

Dancing can be a religious or artistic function or merely an entertainment. But whatever its purpose, the dance is basically an expression of human emotion. It is one of the most beautiful languages used by humans in their efforts to communicate with their fellow beings. It is one of the most profound, perfect joys of life.

The Ancient Greeks and Their Dances

As an expression of fear, sadness, and joy, the dance is as old as civilization. For this reason we cannot know exactly when the Greek dances described in this book actually appeared. We do know, however, that the first documentation of the dance appeared in Homer's epic poems. The dances referred to in his works were performed at various events—at weddings, funerals, symposiums, athletic games, before and after battles. The great poet's descriptions of the charm and ability of the dancers of that period make up some of the most beautiful pages in world literature.

According to Homer, the greatest interpreters of the dance were the Phaeakes (citizens of Corfu), the Trojans, the Mycenaeans, and the Cretans.

If we look into the dance literature of the Classic Period (sixth century B.C.) we will observe that the art of the dance was highly esteemed. With the development of Greek civilization, the Greeks began to discuss the role of the dance and to formulate theories on its relation to society. Dance now became a means of educating, developing, and cultivating the mind and character of the citizen.

The ancient Greeks' love for the dance was such that they believed it had divine origins. Something so beautiful was surely sent by the gods, they

1

reasoned. Thus Terpsichore, the goddess of the dance, became the most cherished of the nine Muses.

The ancient Greeks used dancing for more than expressing emotion. It became a means of exercise, of education for their children, of preparation for soldiers going into battle. Dancing helped young men develop the virtues of a well-rounded adult and soldier—courage, fearlessness, good manners, and love for the noble and beautiful.

Classification of Ancient Greek Dances

As we said previously, the Greeks considered the dance a gift of the gods, and for this reason they combined it with their religious worship. In fact, one of the reasons they felt such happiness when they danced was that they firmly believed the dance was a means of communicating with the gods, that in dancing they were participating in a union with them.

Many of their gods were considered not only excellent teachers of the dance, but fine dancers as well. One legend has it that Rea, the mother of Zeus, was the first to teach dancing to a group of Cretans (the Kourites), while, according to another myth, the goddess Athena invented the famous Pyrrhic war dance.

Plato, who studied, among many other things, the meaning of the dance, concluded that dances could be classified into three main categories: (a) war dances, (b) religious dances, and (c) peace dances.

War Dances

In all probability, war dances, performed before battle to inspire soldiers and prepare them for ultimate victory, are the oldest of all.

Few can say they have not heard of Leonidas and his Spartans at the Battle of Thermopylae. A Persian soldier sent to spy on the Greek camp reported the Spartans' preparations thus:

> They washed and combed their hair, braided wreaths and crowned themselves. They danced—and by God, they certainly did not act as though they were about to go to battle.

The oldest war dance is the dance of the Kourites, whom we mentioned previously. The main characteristic of war dances is that they were performed only by men, bearing weapons.

Dances depicted on an ancient Greek vase.

Religious Dances

Ritual religious dances were performed by both men and women. These were serious, calm, simple dances performed around the altar of the god being honored at a particular ceremony. As they danced, the dancers sang hymns that added to the mysticism of the event.

Contrary to the somberness of most of these dances were those performed for the god Dionysos. The mood of these dances was completely different because Dionysos was considered different from the other gods. This son of Zeus and the mortal Semele was associated with the grapevine and its fruit, which the ancients believed Dionysos gave to mortals as a gift. Many considered Dionysos the god of agriculture, but he was more than that. His influence spread over many areas of the social and religious lives of the ancient Greeks. Most important, he was the symbol of the cycle of life and, as such, he protected the lives of children as they grew into maturity. Because of these varied attributes, Dionysos had numerous worshipers. The rituals of his worship were intense, emotional ceremonies that culminated in ecstatic orgies, for the people believed that as they reached ecstasy, this god took possession of them and they became one with him. The Dionysian worshipers or dancers show the human will to struggle, suffer, and conquer along with their god. For this reason the Dionysian dances are not as somber and gentle as other religious dances. The Dionysian dances were an expression of man's agony and man's love of life on earth.

Pentozali, a Cretan dance (Dora Stratou Dancers).

Peace Dances

Though last in Plato's classification, peace dances were no less important than the others. In fact, they were so varied and numerous that the great philosopher divided them into two categories:

1. Theatrical dances (dances of the theater)
2. Social dances (dances of everyday life)

Theatrical dances derived from the rituals of Dionysos and were performed only in theaters by professionals.

Social dances include the dances performed at symposiums, weddings, funerals, and other social events. The dancers were participants in the event, or professionals who traveled in groups from city to city performing as a means of livelihood. Examples of the latter are the dances of mourning performed at funeral processions.

There is no doubt that today's Greek folk dances are offshoots of the ancient peace dances.

Modern Greeks and Their Dances

Most dances have changed through the years, in some way or other. Some, however, have changed very little. For example, the Cretan *Sousta,* the *Syrtos,* the dances of Cyprus and Thrace, and the Hellenistic *Kalamatianos* have come down to us almost intact. This continuity has led historians to believe that the lives of ancient and modern Greeks are not so different as one might suppose.

British historian T. K. Lawson, who has studied the Greek tradition in detail, says: "A comparison of the character of the ancient and modern Greek is perhaps impossible for the non-Greek who has not known or lived among the Greeks today. Yet no foreigner can look upon a Greek festival without immediately realizing that here before his very eyes are scenes reenacted from ancient days, albeit without their past elegance and dignity."

The festival, or *panagyri* as it is called today, is a miniature of the ancient *Panegyris* in appearance and name. It presents the same mixture of religion, art, trade, athletic meets, and entertainment offered by the Olympic Games of the ancients. Festivals are held on the eve or the very day of the saint's holiday, and usually take place around the saint's church or near some holy or miraculous spring. Art and entertainment at these affairs are represented by the song and the dance.

An Easter festival in Greece.

Dance of Krios-Thrace (Demoglou Dancers).

Every Greek province and village has its own local dance. Of course, they all have many similarities (especially in the rhythm, which is usually 7/8). The mood of each dance and the steps are characteristic of the people of a given area and the geographic nature of their town. The various local dances express the emotions, needs, and desires of the people living in a particular area. The Cretan dances, for instance, are quick, forceful and proud, just like the Cretans who dance them.

On the other hand, the dances performed in the mountain regions are made up of wide steps, high leaps, and heavy stomping on the ground. This is because the pure-spirited Roumeliotes and Arcadians who live in the mountains are rough, daring people.

The dances of the fertile flatlands of Thessaly are calm, unruffled, and proud, like the proud, wealthy Thessalians. In contrast, the people of both northern and southern Epirus dance continuous crossed steps that are monotonous and austere, as though expressing the agony and subjugation these people suffered throughout the many centuries of slavery under the Ottoman

Dance of Salamina (Dora Stratou Dancers).

Empire. These are the dances the enslaved Greeks danced as they fought for freedom on 'the mountains of Greece. To these people, singing and dancing were releases—perhaps the only ones—expressions of their thirst for freedom. They danced and sang proudly, waving their handkerchiefs as though those bits of cloth were their very souls that no power in the world could enslave. They were the souls of the women who died rather than face the Turks at Zalonga.*

Wherever there are Greeks today, they dance proudly, seriously, knowing these dances must be preserved through the centuries. For they are the most real, most beautiful expressions of Greek history and culture, proof of the Greeks' spiritual and ethical worlds, their priceless heritage.

* The Dance of Zalonga has gone down in Greek history as one of the most heroic moments in the revolution against the Turks in 1821. Trapped on a mountain, the women of Zalonga decided to die rather than fall into Turkish hands, where they knew they would be defiled and sold into slavery. They joined hands and danced on the mountaintop toward the edge where, one by one, with their children in tow, they leaped thousands of feet to their death.

Masquerade dance (Dora Stratou Dancers).

Pondiak dance (Demoglou Dancers).

Tsakonic dance (the Labyrinth dance—Dora Stratou Dancers):

The Anastenaria

Traveling through various provinces and villages of Greece, I had the opportunity of learning about the many types of celebrations, customs, and habits of the Greek people. There are customs whose origins we know little about. I was especially impressed with one of the strangest and rarest of these —the Anastenaria, or fire-walking dance, performed by custom on lighted coals. I won't be teaching you this dance and I don't quite recommend that you try it. But it certainly is a fascinating study in faith and the power of mind over matter, so I will tell you about it.

The Anastenaria is an annual event held in certain villages of Thrace and Macedonia (northern Greece), on the feast day of Sts. Constantine and Helen, May 21. It is an ancient Thracean folk custom that refugees brought with them from deep within the Byzantine Empire in Asia Minor. Where and how this custom began have never been clearly explained, but we do know that it stemmed from an idolatry that Christianity could not uproot and finally had to accept. The custom draws worldwide interest and curiosity, and one who views this celebration cannot help but admire and wonder at what unfolds before his eyes. He sees a group of twelve frantic-looking, strangely acting men, one of whom serves as the leader. They all carry icons of Sts. Constantine and Helen adorned with various offerings, including gold and silver pieces and they dance barefoot on lighted coals while praying with a deep faith. They believe that St. Constantine, who is the protector of Christianity and the Anastenarides (literally, those who sigh), will give them strength to confront and route the evil spirit that exists at the gates of their village.

But let us start from the beginning. The event begins with the blessing of the waters at the local village spring. Following this comes the sacrifice of a calf about one year to three years old. This animal sacrifice was practiced by the ancient Greeks. Now the leader of the group appears, followed by the villagers. Together they all march to the leader's home. As the musicians play, the Anastenarides light incense and candles and burn wild flowers while reaching the point of elation. The crowd continues to pray, sing, and dance.

Later in the afternoon, when the excitement has reached its peak, the leader of the Anastenarides gives the sign supposedly received from his leader, St. Constantine, in a spiritual communication. Then, "Fire!" The word passes from mouth to mouth, from person to person, reaching everyone in town and finally to the village square.

Now the procession begins. The barefoot Anastenarides, carrying the saints' icons, the crosses and banners, set out, followed by the band of musicians playing in a steady rhythm, and the crowd of villagers. Singing and dancing their way to the town square, they pause before a huge fire of burning, dry wood sixteen to twenty-one feet in diameter, which lights the surrounding area. When the wood has turned to burning coals, the barefoot Anastenarides follow their leader over the coals, dancing in two directions to form the sign of the cross. The musicians continue playing and the crowd watches and prays while the barefoot Anastenarides, in complete ecstasy, walk and dance over the fire. From time to time other men from the crowd join in, also barefoot, and dance with the Anastenarides over the coals.

In half an hour the coals have turned to ashes under the bare feet of the men. The ritual comes to an end. St. Constantine, protector of the Anastenarides, has protected all good Christians. The dangers and the evil spirits have come and gone. The mysticism remains.

Scientists from all parts of the world, including Greece, have observed the ritual and examined the Anastenarides before and after the event. They can offer no logical or scientific explanation for this phenomenon. There is no injury to the men, no burns on their bare feet.

Villagers carrying the icon of St. Helen walk by the burning coals at the Anastenaria ritual in Langada, Greece;

the firewood is set ablaze;

a villager dances over the burning coals to the music of the village orchestra.

Greek Dances Today

The Greek dances of today are divided into two categories: *traditional folk* dances and *popular folk* dances.

Traditional folk dances come in many varieties but can be subdivided into two basic types: (a) the trailing dances and (b) the leaping dances. Both are performed throughout Greece today, mostly at festivals and national events. They are proud, stalwart dances, performed in a semicircle. When danced in ethnic costumes they are very colorful and effective. The best known of these dances are the Kalamatianos, the Tsamikos, and the Syrtos.

Popular folk dances include the Hassapikos, the Hassaposervikos, and the Zeibekikos.* Though they are called popular folk dances, they actually have little to do with the folk dances of the past. Before World War II, they were performed in rowdy taverns by a tough breed of men called the Koutsavakides (pronounced Koo-tsa-vá-ki-des) or Manges. These were grim, unsmiling individuals, usually drunk on whatever they could obtain at the moment. In their dancing they followed special rules that they took very seriously, so much so that they were known to kill anyone interrupting them as they danced. Knife-wielding was as common to them as breathing.

But World War II changed all this. The outlaws and their dances took on a different character. In the last twenty years, with bouzouki music becoming the latest trend in Greek music, the popular folk dances also became fashionable. Now they are danced everywhere by all classes of Greeks and by foreigners in Greece and abroad. In fact, the dances have become more popular outside of Greece (especially in the United States) than in Athens, which is so cosmopolitan today that it has begun to look down on its folk dances. The popularity of modern rock and disco music has also begun to take its toll.

* The Syrtaki, popular in the United States and Europe, is actually a variation of the Hassapikos, and the Zorba is a variation of the Syrtaki; these two dances were popularized in the film *Zorba the Greek*.

Macedonian dance of the village of Amathia, founded by Alexander the Great (Dora Stratou Dancers).

Greek Costumes

In the past, the Greeks dressed in apparel typical of their home provinces. But when the Greeks adopted Western dress, these clothes became merely costumes to be brought out only when groups performed their national dances. In the three traditional folk dances we are covering, the Greek women wear any local costume they wish, while men wear the traditional foustanella, with its white pleated skirt.

Popular folk dances are never danced in traditional costumes. Dancing groups of this category require men to wear black trousers, white blouses or shirts, and a wide, red sash around their waist. The women wear short skirts and white blouses. You will note this apparel in the photographs in this volume. When you dance these dances for your own pleasure, you will probably wear ordinary clothes. If, however, you wish to hold a Greek party after you have completed your dance course here, it would be very colorful and appropriate if you wore the clothing mentioned above. (See also the chapter "Greek Costumes.")

*Girls from the island of
Corfu dance a wedding dance
with their handkerchiefs
(Dora Stratou Dancers).*

*Macedonian Sohos
dance of Salonica
(Demoglou Dancers).*

18

The Handkerchief in Traditional Folk Dances

Today a handkerchief is a handkerchief, simply that. But in Greek tradition it had a hidden meaning, often contained in a charming story or legend. The handkerchief of the dance was held by a young man and the young lady whom he chose to do the folk dance with him. Often the embroidery on the handkerchief was simply decorative, but it could also be symbolic, expressing the heart's desire of the ladies who embroidered them and danced with them.

This handkerchief of the dance is mentioned many times in traditional songs, and expresses a world of passion, emotion, and special thoughts. It becomes a marriage vow, a secret confession of love, a precious souvenir, and many other things.

Of course, all this occurred at another time and in another place. Today the dancer usually holds a man's white handkerchief for practical reasons: to make turning and twisting easier than it would be if he were holding his partner's hand directly.

The Dances in This Book

I will teach you to dance eight of the most popular Greek dances. First the three traditional dances: Kalamatianos, Tsamikos and Syrtos. Then five popular folk dances: Hassapikos, Hassaposervikos, Syrtaki, Zorba, and Zeibekikos.

You can help me to help you learn these dances if you follow all instructions carefully. Read the details, concentrate, practice, practice, practice . . . and soon these dances will be yours to master.

General Instructions:

1. Learn the basic steps of each dance before beginning the variations.

2. Learn each dance well before going on to the next one. This is **a** must.

3. Count your steps, in equal time at first, to avoid confusion. After you learn the steps, then begin counting according to the rhythm noted on the first page of each dance.

4. Do not use music at first; dance to the music only after you have learned the basic steps and the correct rhythm.

Dance Mood (or Stance):

1. Traditional folk dances are to be danced proudly, happily, holding your head high. You are not trying to show off or tease, but merely to enjoy yourself.

2. Popular folk dances are to be danced with a slight slouch, as though you are tired. Take on an uncaring mood, be a bit thoughtful, pensive, as though you're trying to forget something that is disturbing you.

3. In general, remember that to dance well, freely, you must keep your body in the proper stance regardless of what dance it is. Keep your spine straight and tighten the muscles of your stomach. In this way you control every muscle of your body so that you are dancing and exercising at the same time.

Important Notes:

1. Before you begin, please study carefully the Explanation of Diagrams. Note that after left-to-right steps, the return steps (right-to-left steps)

are drawn above the original left-to-right steps when they should really be danced in the *same line formation* as the original left-to-right steps. For obvious reasons, this cannot be put down on paper.

2.   Note also that in the traditional folk dances, after basic steps and variations, the right foot remains free to continue the dance and does not remain in the starting position as shown in the diagram.

Explanation of Diagrams.

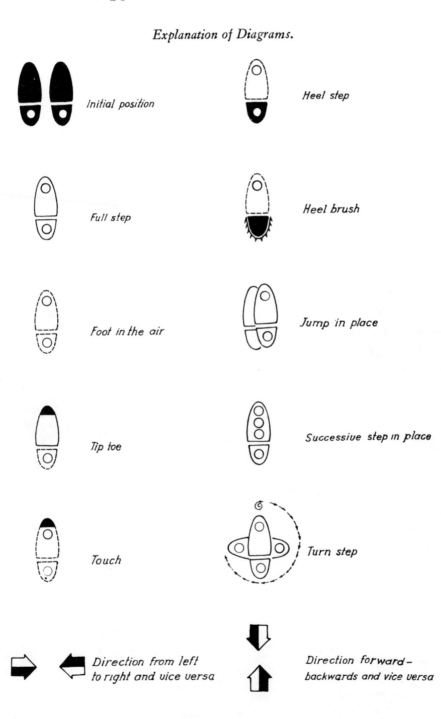

Initial position

Heel step

Full step

Heel brush

Foot in the air

Jump in place

Tip toe

Successive step in place

Touch

Turn step

Direction from left to right and vice versa

Direction forward – backwards and vice versa

Traditional Folk Dances

Make certain you have enough space to practice your steps; use a bare room if possible.

Practice alone or with a group of up to four people. If you are in a group, one person should read the instructions aloud, noting the steps in the diagram, and do the steps while the others follow.

If you learn the dance alone, you should practice later with a group, each person taking a turn as the leader. When he or she completes the variations of the dance just learned, he must relinquish his place to the next person and go to the end of the line. This gives each student a chance to be the leader, and to perform the variations of the dance that are usually done only by the leader.

If you are at a Greek party you might notice different variations of a dance you learned. This is due to the fact that many variations are often improvised. In such cases you should follow the leader with the basic steps of the dance, and when you take over as the leader you may dance the variations you have learned or wish to improvise.

Kalamatianos

Kalamatianos, said to be of ancient origin, is danced throughout Greece by both men and women. The Syrtos or Issos derives from the Kalamatianos. The name of this dance probably originated from a popular folk song, "Kalamatiani," meaning a girl from the province of Kalamata in southern Greece.

The Kalamatianos is danced in a semicircle to the unfamiliar rhythm of 7/8. It consists of twelve basic steps upon which all the variations are based. The variations are performed only by the first, or lead, dancer, who is at the head of the line on the right, facing into the semicircle. All others perform the twelve basic steps repeatedly. However, for better effect any symmetry, school and dance groups performing the Kalamatianos usually have all the dancers do the variations of the dance along with the leader.

Initial Position: Form a semicircle and stand at attention. Dancers join hands at shoulder level with the elbows bent.

Counting the Rhythm:
Steps:

1	slow
2–3	fast
4	slow
5–6	fast
7	slow
8–9	fast
10	slow
11–12	fast

Greater emphasis is placed on steps 1, 4, 7, and 10.

Kalamatianos – Basic Steps.

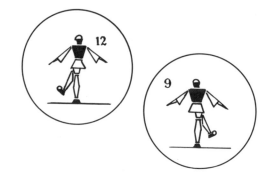

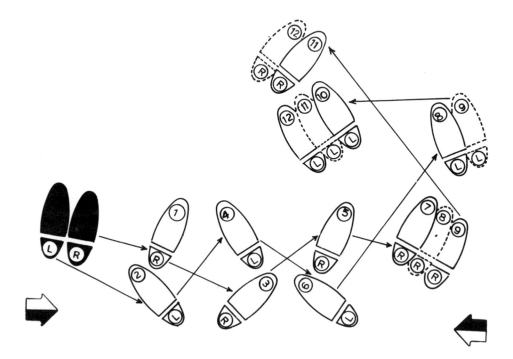

Kalamatianos

Basic Steps: 12

Music: 7/8

The leader and the second dancer (to the leader's left) hold a man's white handkerchief between them.

Step   1*:   Step to the right with right foot.

Step   2 :   Cross left foot behind right foot.

Step   3 :   Step to the right with right foot.

Step   4 :   Cross left foot in front of right foot.

Step   5 :   Step to the right with right foot.

Step   6 :   Cross left foot behind right foot.

Step   7 :   Stamp right foot to the right; simultaneously turn and face right, away from the semicircle.

Step   8 :   Cross the left foot in front of the right foot and raise the right foot slightly.

Step   9 :   Return the right foot to its previous position and slightly raise the left leg forward, knee straight.

Step 10*:   Stamp the left foot to the left; simultaneously turn and face left in the direction of the semicircle.

Step 11 :   Cross the right foot in front of left foot and raise the left foot slightly.

Step 12 :   Return the left foot to its previous position and slightly raise the right leg forward, knee straight.

These are the twelve basic steps of the Kalamatianos. You may repeat them as often as you wish before starting the variations.

Note: As the leader dances the variations, he should insert, from time to time, the basic steps in order to keep the line moving. (When the leader performs the variations in any dance, the rest of the line is slowed down,

* Denotes accented step.

often just keeping step in the same spot as the leader performs his leaps, etc.) Although the following variations all begin with the dancer standing at attention, feet together, in practice each variation can continue from the last position of the previous one.

The first two variations of the Kalamatianos are so simple I feel they do not require a diagram.

1st Variation — Kalamatianos

Step 1*:   Face left in the direction of the semicircle and place the right foot behind the left.

Step 2 :   Place the left foot behind the right.

Steps 3, 4,* 5, 6:   Repeat the first two steps twice, still facing left in the direction of the semicircle.

Steps 7,* 8, 9, 10, 11, 12:   These are identical to basic steps 6 through 12.

2nd Variation — Kalamatianos

Step 1*:   Face left in the direction of the semicircle and place the right foot behind the left.

Step 2 :   Place the left foot behind the right.

Step 3 :   Step to the right with the right foot, and immediately:

Step 4*:   Cross the left foot in front of the right foot.

Step 5 :   Repeat step 1.

Step 6 :   Repeat step 2.

Steps 7,* 8, 9, 10, 11, 12:   These are identical to basic steps 6 through 12.

The Kalamatianos (Demoglou Dancers).

Kalamatianos − 3rd Variation.

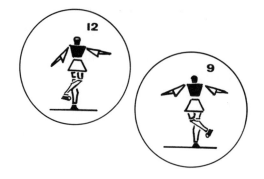

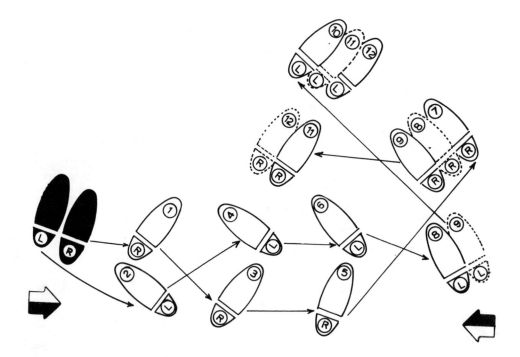

3rd Variation — Kalamatianos

Steps 1,* 2, 3, 4,* and 5:   These are identical to basic steps 1 through 5.

Step   6 :   Cross the left foot in front of the right.

Step   7*:   Step to the right with the right foot, simultaneously turn and face left, in the direction of the semicircle.

Step   8 :   Cross the left foot behind the right and raise the right foot slightly.

Step   9 :   Return the right foot to its previous position and raise the left foot slightly.

Step 10*:   Step to the left with the left foot, simultaneously turn and face right, away from the semicircle.

Step 11 :   Cross the right foot behind the left and raise the left foot slightly.

Step 12 :   Return the left foot to its previous position and raise the right foot slightly.

Kalamatianos – 4th Variation.

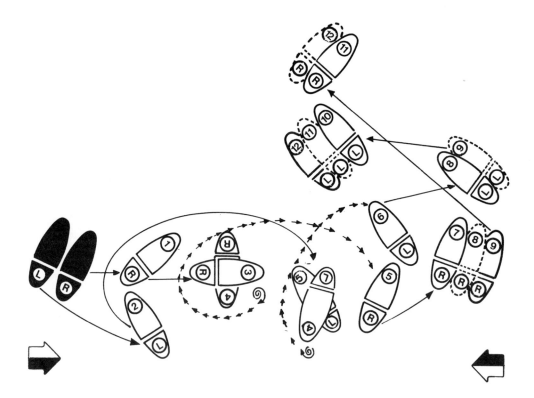

4th Variation – Kalamatianos

Right Turn

Steps 1 and 2: These are identical to the basic steps 1 and 2.

Step 3: Step to the right with the right foot; simultaneously turn and face right.

Step 4: Using the right leg as the pivot, turn right until you face in the opposite direction from which you began. Bring the left foot next to the right foot.

Step 5: Using the left leg as the pivot, continue turning right until you face front once again. End the turn by stepping to the right with the right foot.

Step 6: Cross the left foot in front of the right.

Steps 7, 8, 9, 10,* 11, and 12:* These are identical to the last basic steps.

Note: You may make more than one turn if you wish. For two turns, begin with the first two basic steps and turn twice until step 7. Finish with the last five basic steps. For three turns, begin turning at step 1 and continue turning until step 7. Again, finish with the last five basic steps. You may also make a left turn at the last three steps: 10, 11, and 12, as follows:

Step 10: Step to the left with the left foot; simultaneously turn and face left (prepare for complete turn).

Step 11: Using the left leg as the pivot, turn left until you face in the opposite direction from which you began. Bring the right foot in front of the left.

Step 12: Using the right leg as the pivot, continue turning left until you face front once again quickly and lower foot in place.

Kalamatianos – 5th Variation.

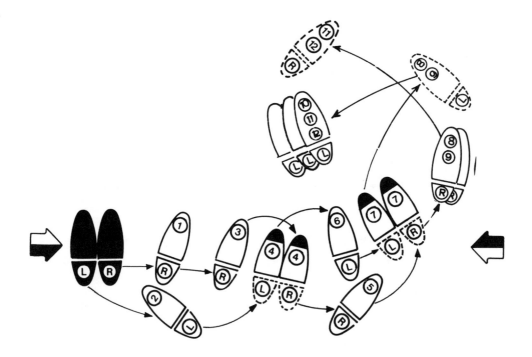

5th Variation – Kalamatianos

Squat at Steps 4 and 7

Steps 1, 2, and 3:*   These are identical to the first three basic steps.

Step   4*:   Jump in place, bringing both feet together, and land in a squat, on the balls of both feet.

Step   5 :   Rise, stepping to the right with the right foot.

Step   6 :   Cross the left foot in front of the right.

Step   7*:   Jump in place, bringing both feet together, and land in a squat as in step 4.

Step   8 :   Rise, hopping on the right foot, toward the right; at the same time raise the left leg, knee bent, in front of the right.

Step   9 :   Hop in place on the right foot.

Step 10 :   Step to the left with the left foot.

Step 11 :   Hop on the left foot; at the same time, raise the right leg, knee bent, in front of the left.

Step 12 :   Hop in place on the left foot.

Note: You may add or subtract a squat—that is, you may squat only on step 4 and continue with basic steps 5 through 12; or you may squat on the first step and make three more squats, as follows:

Step   1*:   Squat.

Step   2 :   Rise and hop on the right foot, in place, raising the left leg back, knee bent.

Step   3 :   Hop on the left foot, in place, raising the right leg back, knee bent. (In other words, you take three steps—one squat and two hops. Repeat these three steps three more times to complete the twelve steps.)

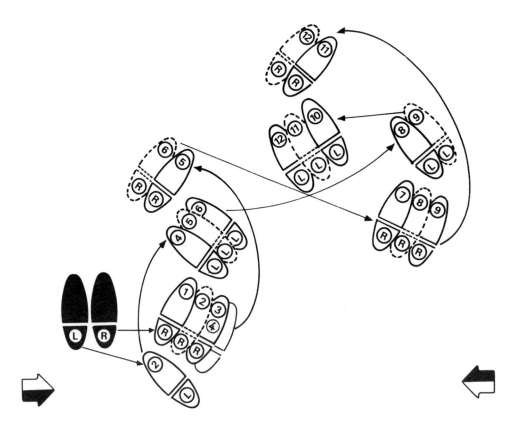

34

6th Variation – Kalamatianos

Cross Steps in Place

Step 1:   Step to the right with the right foot.

Step 2:   Cross the left foot behind the right, and raise the right foot slightly.

Step 3:   Return the right foot to its previous position.

Step 4:   Hop on the right foot, bringing the left foot down in front of the right.

Step 5:   Jump in place, crossing the right foot in front of the left as you land, and raise the left foot slightly.

Step 6:   Jump in place, bringing the left foot down behind the right as you land, and raise the right foot slightly.

Steps 7, 8, 9, 10, 11, and 12:   Repeat the last six basic steps.

Kalamatianos – 7th Variation.

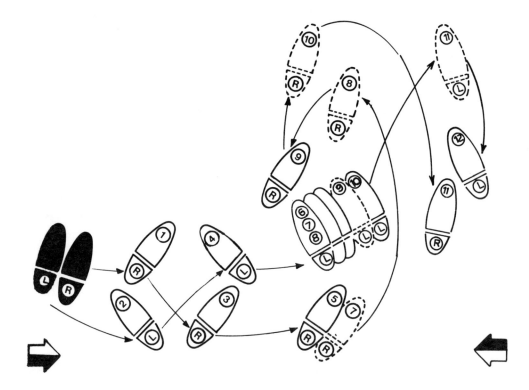

7th Variation – Kalamatianos

Men's Scissors Step

Steps 1,* 2, 3, 4,* and 5:   These are identical to first five basic steps.

Step 6:   Cross the left foot in front of the right.

Step 7:   Hop on the left foot and simultaneously raise the right leg back, with the knee bent.

Step 8:   Repeat hop on the left foot and simultaneously swing the right leg forward in the air, with the knee straight.

Step 9:   Cross the right foot in front of the left and slightly raise the left leg.

Step 10:   Stamp the left foot in place and simultaneously raise the leg forward in the air with the knee straight. Now we are ready for the scissors step to the right.

Step 11:   Jump to the right in the following manner: Make a large circle in the air with your right leg; simultaneously make an identical circle with your left leg. For an instant, the left leg crosses over the right leg in the air. Land on the right foot. The left leg remains raised forward in the air with the knee straight.

Step 12:   Bring the left foot down quickly, crossing it in front of the right.

Note: Steps 11 and 12 follow one another almost instantly. This is a difficult variation: Getting the legs to cross over in midair requires a good deal of practice.

Kalamatianos

San ___ pas sti ka la ma ta ke this me to ___ ka lo fe-

ee-me na nyau ti ___ li na va-lo sto le mo ___ San mo ___

FINE

39

Syrtos

The Syrtos or Issos is a very old Greek dance preserved from antiquity. Some claim that it stems from the Kalamatianos, but others assert that it is the oldest of all the Greek dances with religious origins lost in antiquity. (Incidentally, the ancient Greeks called all circular dances Syrtos.)

This dance is well known throughout Greece and is performed by both men and women.

The beat of Syrtos is 2/4, and it has twelve basic steps with many variations. The variations are danced only by the leader of the group. The others repeatedly dance the twelve basic steps as all circular dances.

The initial position of Syrtos is the same as that of Kalamatianos.

Dancing the Syrtos at a Greek festival.

Counting the Rhythm:

Steps:

1	slow
2–3	fast
4	slow
5–6	fast
7	slow
8–9	fast
10	slow
11–12	fast

Greater emphasis is placed on steps 1, 4, 7, and 10.

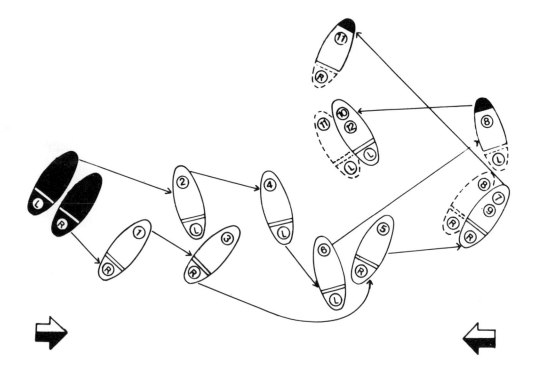

Syrtos

Basic Steps: 12

Music: 2/4

Step   1*:   Step to the right with the right foot.

Step   2 :   Cross the left foot in front of the right.

Step   3 :   Brush the right foot to the heel of the left foot. (This is a small step.)

Step   4*:   Cross the left foot in front of the right.

Step   5 :   Step to the right with the right foot.

Step   6 :   Brush the left foot to the heel of the right foot. (This is a small step.)

Step   7*:   Step to the right with the right foot.

Step   8 :   Cross the left foot in front of the right and slightly raise the right foot. (The weight of the body rests on the ball of the left foot slightly off the ground.)

Step   9 :   Return the right foot to its previous position.

Step 10*:   Step to the left with the left foot.

Step 11 :   Cross the right foot in front of the left (the weight of the body rests on the ball of the right foot with the heel slightly off the ground) and slightly raise the left foot.

Step 12 :   Return the left foot to its previous position.

Syrtos — 1st Variation.

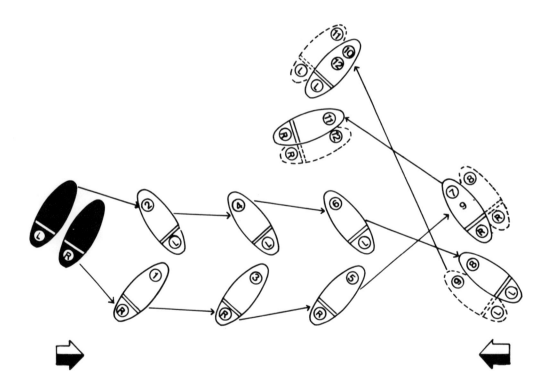

1st Variation — Syrtos

Brush Crossings

Step 1*:   Step to the right with the right foot.

Step 2 :   Brush the left foot in front of the right foot.

Step 3 :   Repeat step 1.

Step 4*:   Repeat step 2.

Step 5 :   Repeat step 1.

Step 6 :   Repeat step 2.

Step 7*:   Step to the right with the right foot; simultaneously turn and face left in the direction of the semicircle.

Step 8 :   Cross the left foot behind the right and raise the right foot slightly.

Step 9 :   Return the right foot to its previous position and raise the left foot slightly.

Step 10*:   Step to the left with the left foot, simultaneously turn and face right, away from the semicircle.

Step 11 :   Cross the right foot behind the left, and raise the left foot slightly.

Step 12 :   Return the left foot to its previous position, and raise the right foot slightly.

Syrtos — 2nd Variation.

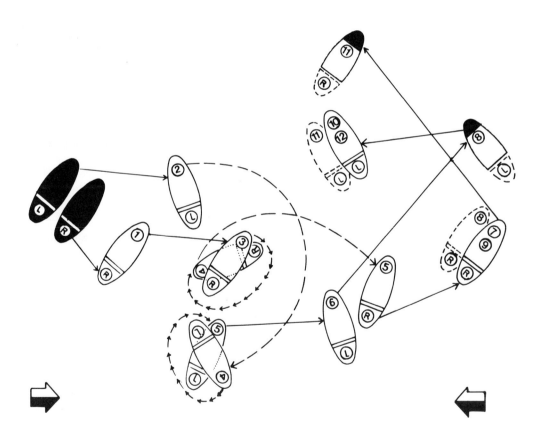

46

2nd Variation – Syrtos

Right Turn

Steps 1,* 2, and 3:   These are identical to the first three basic steps.

Step 4*:   Using the right leg as the pivot, turn right until you face in the opposite direction from which you began. Bring the left foot in front of the right.

Step 5 :   Using the left leg as the pivot, turn to the right until you are facing front once again. End the turn by stepping to the right with the right foot.

Step 6 :   Brush the left foot to the heel of the right foot. (This is a small step.)

Steps 7,* 8, 9, 10,* 11, and 12:   These are identical to the last six basic steps.

Syrtos — 3rd Variation.

3rd Variation — Syrtos

Cross Step to the Center and Back

Step 1*:   Step to the right with the right foot.

Step 2 :   Cross the left foot behind the right.

Step 3 :   Brush the right foot to the right.

Step 4 :   Brush the left foot to the right, crossing it in front of the right foot.

Step 5 :   Brush the right foot to the right.

Step 6 :   Brush the left foot to the right, crossing it in front of the right foot.

Step 7*:   Bring the right foot in front of the left in a half-circle motion.

Step 8 :   Bring the left foot in front of the right in a half-circle motion.

Step 9 :   Brush the right foot to the heel of the left.

Step 10 :   Bring the left foot behind the right, without turning. (This is a back step.)

Step 11 :   Bring the right foot behind the left, without turning. (This is a back step.)

Step 12 :   Brush the left foot back, bringing its heel close to the arch of the right foot. (This is a small step.)

Note: In steps 7, 8, and 9, we face front and move forward. In steps 10, 11, and 12, we move back to our original position in the line, still facing front.

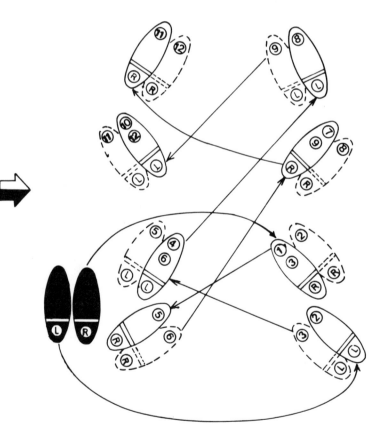

4th Variation – Syrtos

Side Cross Steps to the Right and Left

Step 1: Step to the right with the right foot; simultaneously turn and face left.

Step 2: Cross the left foot behind the right and raise the right foot slightly.

Step 3: Return the right foot to its previous position and raise the left foot slightly.

Step 4: Step to the left with the left foot; simultaneously turn and face right.

Step 5: Cross the right foot behind the left and raise the left foot slightly.

Step 6: Return the left foot to its previous position and raise the right foot slightly.

Step 7: Step to the right with the right foot.

Step 8: Cross the left foot in front of the right and raise the right foot slightly.

Step 9: Return the right foot to its previous position and raise the left foot slightly.

Step 10: Step to the left with the left foot; simultaneously turn and face left.

Step 11: Cross the right foot in front of the left and raise the left foot slightly.

Step 12: Return the left foot to its previous position and raise the right foot slightly.

Note: These steps are performed left and right, in place. The knee should be slightly bent whenever the foot is raised.

Syrtos

53

Members of the Licion Hellinidon Dance Group of Greece performing a variation of the Tsamikos.

Tsamikos

The Tsamikos is an imposing dance whose rhythm is one of grandeur. Its variations consist of both smooth and leaping steps, which give the dance a triumphant air, making it the handsomest of the Greek dances.

In earlier times the Tsamikos was danced in mountainous areas only by men. Today it is a pan-Hellenic dance performed by men and women.

Its name derives from the Tsamides, the people who lived during the seventeenth and eighteenth centuries in the area of Tsamouria in Epirus, in northern Greece. It is also called Kleftikos because it was danced by the fighters and rebels (Klefts) of the Greek Revolution of 1821 against the Turks. After battle, the Greek fighters would relax by holding dance competitions and games as means of entertainment.

The number of steps in the Tsamikos varies according to the area where it is danced, and according to the song accompanying the dance. It usually begins with a minimum of ten steps; the popular version danced throughout Greece contains twelve steps. A sixteen-step version is danced mostly by dance groups where all the dancers perform both the basic steps and the variations.

The Tsamikos is danced in a semicircle. The leader performs the variations while the others follow with the basic steps, except in the sixteen-step version as noted previously.

The Tsamikos performed by the Demoglou Dancers.

Tsamikos – Basic Steps (12-Step Version).

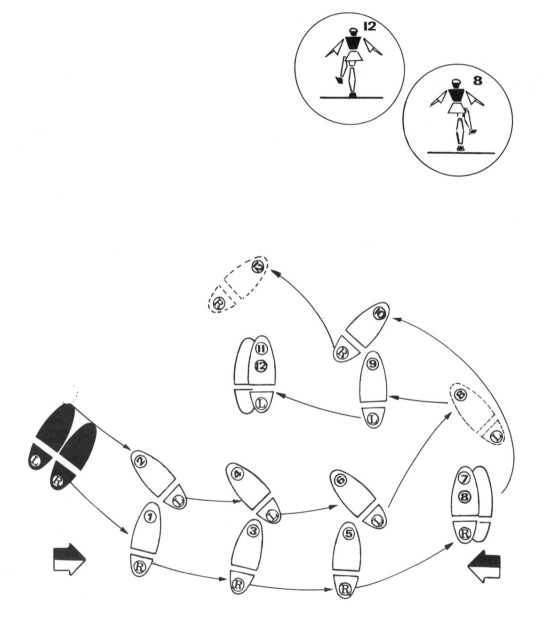

12-Step Version — Tsamikos

Basic Steps: 12

Music: 3/8

Initial Position: The Tsamikos' initial position is exactly the same as that of the Kalamatianos. Form a semicircle and stand at attention. Dancers join hands at shoulder level, with the elbows bent.

Counting the Rhythm:

Steps 1, 3, 5, 7, 9, and 11 are emphasized in beat—they take twice the time of the even-numbered steps.

Step 1:   Step to the right with the right foot.

Step 2:   Cross the left foot in front of the right.

Step 3:   Repeat step 1.

Step 4:   Repeat step 2.

Step 5:   Repeat step 1.

Step 6:   Repeat step 2.

Step 7:   Stamp the right foot to the right.

Step 8:   Hop on the right foot and simultaneously raise the left leg, knee bent, in front of the right.

Step 9:   Step to the left with the left foot.

Step 10:   Cross the right foot in front of the left.

Step 11:   Stamp the left foot to the left.

Step 12:   Hop on the left foot and raise the right leg, knee bent, in front of the left.

Note: The leading dancer should often insert the basic steps between variations.

Tsamikos – Basic Steps (16-Step Version).

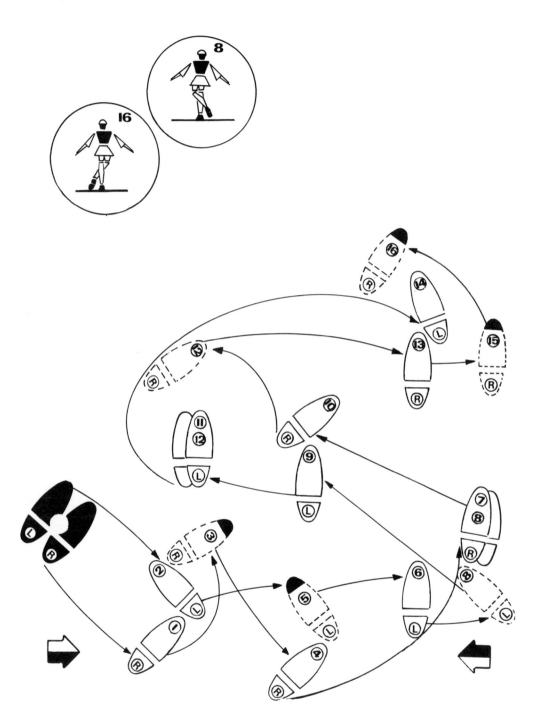

16-Step Version — Tsamikos

Basic Steps: 16

Step   1:   Step to the right with the right foot.

Step   2:   Cross the left foot in front of the right.

Step   3:   Bring the right foot on tiptoe in front of the left. (Weight rests on the left foot.)

Step   4:   Step to the right with the right foot.

Step   5:   Bring the left foot on tiptoe in front of the right. (Weight rests on the right foot.)

Step   6:   Step to the right with the left foot. (The left leg is crossed in front of the right.)

Step   7:   Stamp the right foot to the right.

Step   8:   Hop on the right foot and simultaneously raise the left leg back, with the knee bent.

Step   9:   Step to the left with the left foot.

Step 10:   Cross the right foot in front of the left.

Step 11:   Stamp the left foot to the left.

Step 12:   Hop on the left foot and simultaneously raise the right, knee bent, leg in front of the left.

Step 13:   Step to the right with the right foot.

Step 14:   Cross the left foot in front of the right.

Step 15:   Make a small step to the right with the right foot on tiptoe.

Step 16:   Cross the right foot on tiptoe in front of the left.

Note: The Tsamikos variations that follow are performed in twelve steps. However, in case the music playing requires sixteen steps, you should add basic steps 13, 14, 15, and 16 above.

Tsamikos – 1st Variation.

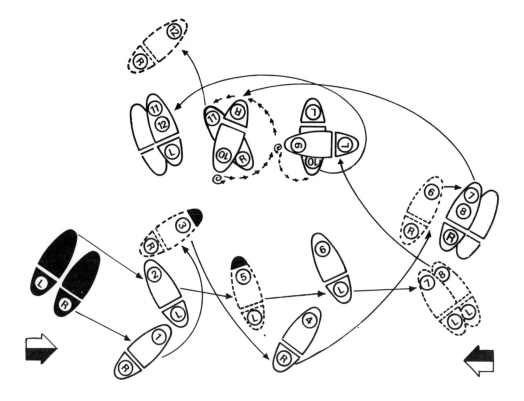

1st Variation – Tsamikos

Right Kick

Steps 1, 2, 3, 4, and 5: These are identical to the first five basic steps in the sixteen-step version.

Step 6: The left foot is on tiptoe. Step to the right with the left foot and simultaneously kick the right leg to the right. (This is a jumping step.)

Step 7: Jump to the right; as you land on the right foot, raise the left leg back, with knee bent.

Step 8: Hop in place on the right foot.

Step 9: Prepare for a left turn. Step to the left with the left foot, simultaneously turn, and face left.

Step 10: Using the left leg as the pivot, turn left until you face in the opposite direction from which you began. Bring the right foot close to the left.

Step 11: Using the right leg as the pivot, continue turning toward the left until you face front once again. End the turn by stepping to the left with the left foot.

Step 12: Raise the right leg, knee bent, in front of the left as you hop on the left foot.

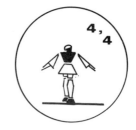

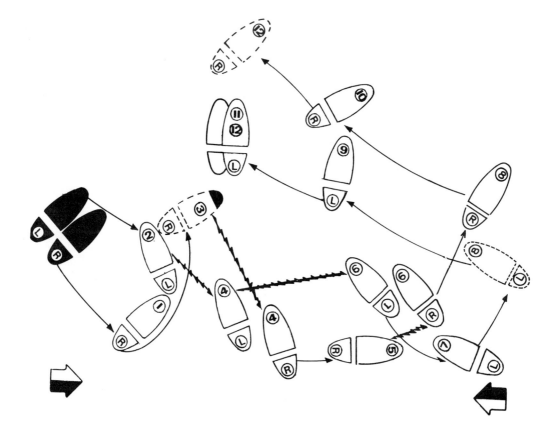

2nd Variation — Tsamikos

Double Slide

Steps 1, 2, and 3:   These are identical to first three basic steps in the sixteen-step version.

Step 4:   Double step: As you turn the body to the left, (a) brush the right foot back, and (b) brush the left foot in front of the right. (These are small steps done in rapid succession.)

Step 5:   Step to the right with the right foot as you turn the body slightly toward your right.

Step 6:   Double step: As your turn the body slightly toward your left, (a) brush the left foot in front of the right and (b) brush the right foot behind the left. Again, these are small steps done in rapid succession.

Step 7:   Bring the left foot behind the right foot.

Step 8:   Jump to the right with the right foot; simultaneously raise the left leg back with the knee bent.

Steps 9, 10, 11, and 12:   Do the last four basic steps in the twelve-step version dancing to the left. Or make a complete turn to the left as in the first variation.

Tsamikos – 3rd Variation.

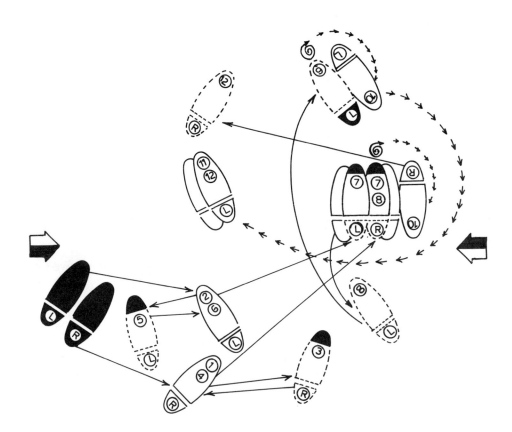

3rd Variation — Tsamikos

Squat, Heel Turn

Step 1: Step to the right with the right foot.

Step 2: Cross the left foot in front of the right.

Step 3: Bring the right foot on tiptoe to the right. (Weight rests on the left foot.)

Step 4: Cross the right foot behind the left.

Step 5: Bring the left foot on tiptoe to the left. (Weight rests on the right foot.)

Step 6: Cross the left foot in front of the right.

Step 7: The squat step: Jump to the right, bringing both feet together, and land in a squat, placing all your weight on the balls of both feet.

Step 8: Rise, hopping on the right foot; at the same time raise the left leg back, with the knee bent.

Step 9: Bring the left foot down in front of the right foot so that only the heel touches the floor.

Step 10: Prepare for a complete turn by shifting the weight of the body forward to the left leg, knee straight. Using the left leg as the pivot and slightly raising the right foot, turn to the right in place until you are facing in the opposite direction from which you began. At the end of this half turn, the right foot will be in front of the left.

Step 11: Using the right leg as the pivot and slightly raising the left foot, continue turning until you face front once again. End the turn by stepping to the left with the left foot.

Step 12: Hop on the left foot and raise the right leg, knee bent, in front of the left.

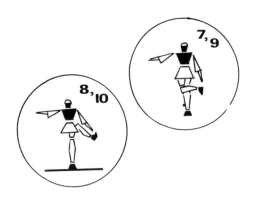

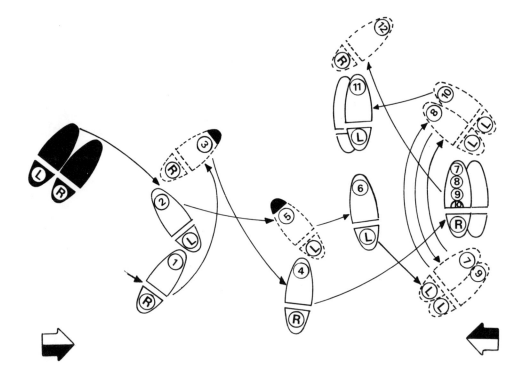

4th Variation — Tsamikos

Steps 1, 2, 3, 4, 5, and 6: These are identical to the first six basic steps in the sixteen-step version.

Step 7: Jump to the right and land on the right foot, simultaneously raising the left leg back, with the knee bent. Tap the left toes with the right hand. (The right knee is also slightly bent.)

Step 8: Hop on the right foot, simultaneously swinging the left leg, knee bent, in front of the right. Tap the left toes with the right hand.

Step 9: Hop on the right foot, simultaneously swinging the left leg, knee bent, behind the right, and tap the toes again.

Step 10: Repeat step 8.

Step 11: Step to the left with the left foot.

Step 12: Raise the right leg, knee bent, in front of the left, and tap the right toes with the left hand.

Note: Before you tap the right toes with the left hand, release the hand of the dancer on your left. Hold hands again as soon as tapping is over.

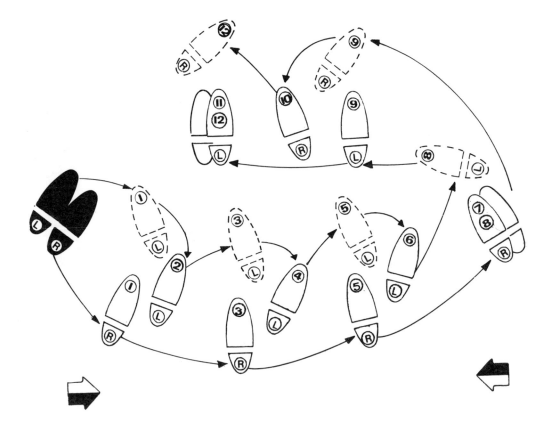

5th Variation – Tsamikos

Scissors Steps

Step 1: Jump to the right and land on the right foot, simultaneously raising the left leg, knee straight, in front of the right. (This is called the scissors step.)

Step 2: Bring the left foot down, crossing it in front of the right.

Step 3: Repeat step 1 (the scissors step) to the right.

Step 4: Bring the left foot down, crossing it in front of the right.

Step 5: Repeat step 1 (the scissors step) to the right.

Step 6: Bring the left foot down, crossing it in front of the right.

Step 7: Stamp the right foot to the right.

Step 8: Hop on the right foot, simultaneously raising the left leg, knee bent, in front of the right.

Step 9: Jump to the left and land on the left foot, simultaneously raising the right leg, knee straight, in front of the left (the scissors step).

Step 10: Bring the right foot down, crossing it in front of the left.

Step 11: Stamp the left foot to the left.

Step 12: Hop on the left foot, simultaneously raising the right leg, knee bent, in front of the left.

Note: During the first three scissors steps (steps 1 to 5 in this variation) you may also do three turns to the right and tap the toes of left foot with the right hand. Turns and taps take place in steps 1, 3, and 5. But in steps 9 and 10, the dancer may make the left turns without tapping the toes.

Tsamikos

Tsamikos danced by Evzones (Demoglou Dancers).

A traditional Greek orchestra (clarinet, violin, santouri, and lauto).

Demotic or Traditional Music

Another basic mark of the Greek people, as characteristic of their traditional dances, is the demotic* or traditional music that has played an important role in their lives since ancient times. The theory of Greek music is based on Pythagoras' theory of acoustics. With a single-string instrument, Pythagoras (582–505 B.C.) defined the mathematical spacing of the music scales and set the basis for our musical system.

In the religious field, the Byzantine and post-Byzantine liturgy carried on a musical tradition over fifteen hundred years old. Even today Byzantine ecclesiastical music is sung and played as purely as in the time it was written.

Demotic or traditional Greek music, which consists of the immortal Greek patriotic songs, is as highly valued as Greek religious music and is closely related to the traditional dances.

The popular folk songs and neo-Hellenic music are a blend of Byzantine and traditional music with other elements, and are closely related to the popular folk dances. The traditional folk song and its music took root between the sixth and tenth centuries A.D., in the areas of Kapadokias and Pontos in Asia Minor, where the Akritans lived. (Akritans were those who guarded the frontier borders of the Byzantine Empire.) After the fall of Constantinople to the Turks in 1453, and the destruction of the Byzantine Empire, Greece lived the most tragic days of her history. The four hundred years of Turkish (Ottoman) rule that followed prevented any cultural or intellectual growth, and the folk song was transformed, taking on a Middle Eastern flavor (the *amané*).

The real growth of the folk song began in the eighteenth century, when the Greeks began to conceive the idea of eventual freedom from Turkish occupation, and reached its peak during the last years before the Revolution of 1821. In general, the themes of the Greek folk songs were the lives of the enslaved Greeks and their struggle for independence.

*From the Greek words *demos* (people) and *demotico* (of the people).

The Demotic or Traditional Folk Orchestra

The musical instruments making up the demotic orchestra are divided into three groups: string, wind, and percussion.

STRING INSTRUMENTS

Laouto: A type of guitar that comes in many forms, popular since the Middle Ages.

Oud: A rounded guitar used since the Middle Ages.

Santouri: A string instrument in the shape of a small rectangle used as first accompaniment.

Lyre: An instrument of the ancient Greeks, in the shape of a small violin, found in Crete today.

Above, carved lyres from the island of Crete.

Opposite, a Greek peasant boy playing the flute.

WIND INSTRUMENTS

Flogera: A type of flute, made of bamboo, bronze, aluminum, or the foot of a fowl, and often made by shepherds.

Karamouza: A type of flute usually made from a pig's bladder.

PERCUSSION INSTRUMENTS

Daouli: A rhythm instrument (drum) made from the skin of sheep or goats.

Toumbaneli: A small drum.

Defi: A tambourine.

(The last two are usually played by the singers.)

The above instruments were used by the Greeks in open spaces. The European clarinet appeared in Greece in 1835, and its sound soon replaced that of the *flogera,* the *karamouza,* and the *daouli.*

These latter instruments, suitable only for the outdoors because of their far-reaching sounds, had no place in closed quarters. For this reason they drifted into the background. The same occurred with the lyre, which, in many cases, was replaced by the violin.

It is admirable that the talented men who played these instruments were self-taught, creating through experience their own technique, which merged with the aesthetics of folk music and the character of the folk dance.

Fisherman's dance performed by the Dora Stratou Dancers.

Popular Folk Dances

We now come to the popular folk dances, which, as we said, are different from the traditional or demotic dances in appearance and in the way they are danced.

Four of the five popular folk dances that follow are performed with two or more people in a straight line, holding each other's shoulders.

All the variations of these dances are danced by the whole group and not just by the leader, as in the traditional dances.

The leader or first dancer in the popular folk dances is the one who knows the variations best. He or she always dances at the right end and often whispers a reminder to the others of what the next variation will be.

The fifth popular folk dance, the Zeibekoko, is completely different from the other dances in this book, as you will observe farther on. You may learn this alone, since it is a dance that can be performed by a simple dancer.

Note: Practice popular folk dancing in groups of two or more. If you and your friends attend various Greek social affairs often it will be better to study the dances together, so you may do the dances in unison. If this is difficult, you may study in groups of twos, but at the earliest opportunity you should practice in a larger group.

Do this over and over until you learn the dances correctly and uniformly. To make it easier for you to tie in one variation with another, I am showing the last step of the previous variation at the beginning of the next one.

Hassapikos

We know very little of the origin of the Hassapikos except that it was a very old dance performed by the Greek butchers of old Byzantium. (The Greek word for butcher is *hassapis;* hence the name.) Before World War II the Hassapikos was performed only by men, mostly on the islands and in ports. But today, with bouzouki music so popular, the Hassapikos is also danced by women and has become an international dance.

It is danced in a straight line, with each dancer holding the shoulders of his partners. The dancers hunch their backs slightly while bending their knees. This is probably due to the fact that the butchers who danced in the *tavernas* after a hard day's work were bent and tired from their labors. For this reason, too, they held each other up by the shoulders as they danced this favorite of theirs.

The Hassapikos is performed by two or more dancers who execute identical steps. It has many variations, and every dancer follows the one he believes to be best. For this reason this dance is difficult to dance with more than two persons unless they have all practiced the same steps together at a previous time. Students of this dance should all learn from the same teacher and should co-ordinate their steps in advance. It is the only way to present it in all its beauty, for it is undeniably one of the handsomest dances Greece offers today.

Demoglou Dancers performing the Hassapikos.

Each Hassapikos variation begins with the last position of the preceding variation (or in the case of the first variation, with the last position of the basic sequences).

Hassapikos

Hassapikos – Basic Steps.

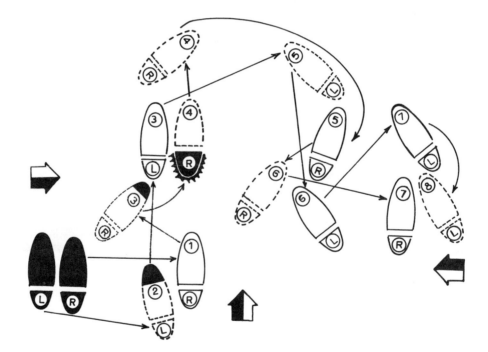

Hassapikos

Basic Steps: 8

Music: 2/4

Initial Position: Dancers stand at attention in a straight line and place their hands on the shoulders of the dancers on either side. Be sure to keep the extended arms straight and stiff.

Step 1: Step to the right with the right foot.

Step 2: Bring the left foot on tiptoe next to the right foot.

Step 3: Step forward on the left foot, body leaning forward and both knees bent; simultaneously tap the floor with the right toes, close behind the left heel.

Step 4: Brush the right heel alongside the left foot and immediately move the right leg, knee bent, up and down in front of the left leg without touching the floor. (This is in effect a downward kick in the air.)

Step 5: Bring the right foot down behind the left; quickly raise the left leg, kicking downward as in step 4.

Step 6: Bring the left foot down behind the right and kick the right leg to the left.

Step 7: Step to the right with the right foot and simultaneously brush the left foot in front of the right. Both knees should be slightly bent, the weight of the body resting on the left foot.

Step 8: Pull back, shifting the weight of the body to the right foot; simultaneously bring the left foot (toes pointing down and off the floor) in front of the right leg.

Note: Steps 3–7 each involve two movements in one beat. These movements should be done in rapid succession.

Hassapikos – 1st Variation.

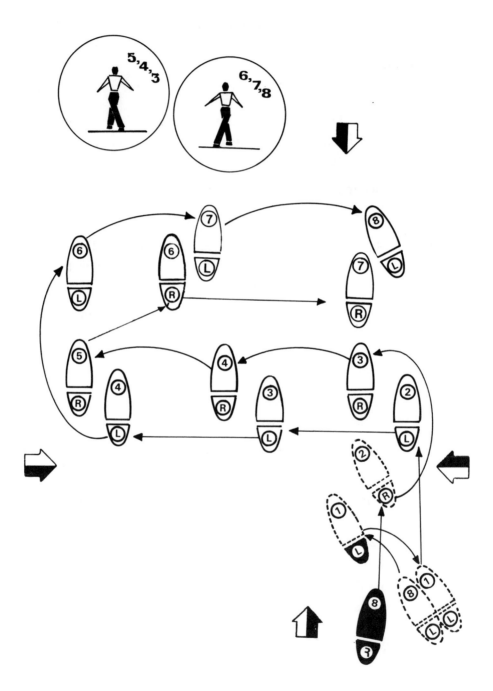

1st Variation – Hassapikos*

Three Cross Steps to the Left
Three Cross Steps to the Right

Step 1: Stand as in basic step 8. Quickly touch the floor in front of the right foot with the left heel; immediately return the left foot to its previous position.

Step 2: Step forward on the left foot, body leaning forward and left knee bent; simultaneously bring the right foot (toes pointing down and slightly off the floor) close behind the heel of the left foot.

Step 3: Bring the right foot forward and cross it in front of the left in a half-circle motion. Immediately brush the left foot to the left.

Step 4: Cross the right foot in front of the left. Immediately brush the left foot to the left.

Step 5: Cross the right foot in front of the left. Weight rests on the right leg, knee slightly bent.

Step 6: Bring the left foot forward and cross it in front of the right in a half-circle motion. Immediately brush the right foot to the right.

Step 7: Cross the left foot in front of the right. Immediately brush the right foot to the right.

Step 8: Cross the left foot in front of the right. Weight rests on the left leg, knee slightly bent.

*After each variation return to the basic steps for one or two sequences before starting another variation.

Hassapikos – 2nd Variation.

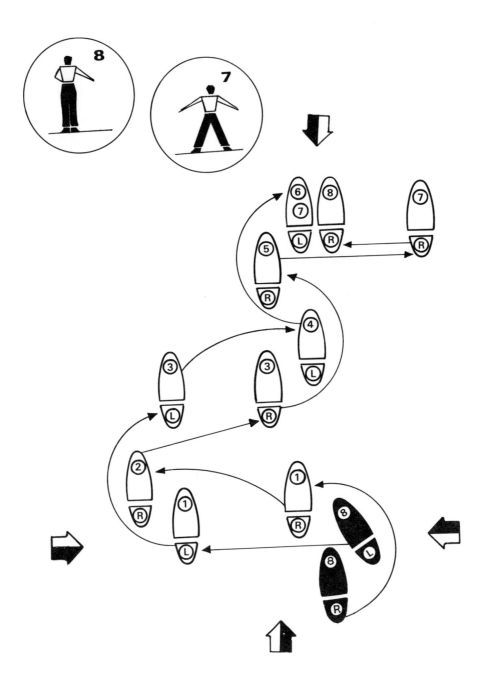

2nd Variation — Hassapikos

Two Cross Steps to the Left
Two Cross Steps to the Right
Two Steps Forward, Balance, and Close

These cross steps are identical to the cross steps of the first variation.

Step 1: Bring the right foot forward and cross it in front of the left in a half-circle motion. Immediately brush the left foot to the left.

Step 2: Cross the right foot in front of the left. Weight rests on right leg, knee slightly bent.

Step 3: Bring the left foot forward and cross it in front of the right in a half-circle motion. Immediately brush the right foot to the right.

Step 4: Cross the left foot in front of the right. Weight rests on the left foot, knee slightly bent.

Step 5: Bring the right foot forward and cross it in front of the left in a half-circle motion.

Step 6: Bring the left foot forward and cross it in front of the right in a half-circle motion.

Step 7: Step to the right with the right foot and immediately sway to the right and to the left.

Step 8: Brush the right foot next to the left and stand at attention.

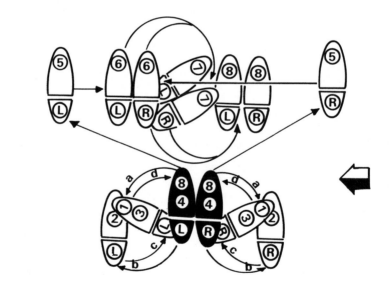

3rd Variation – Hassapikos

Open Toes and Heels
Closed Toes and Heels

Step 1: You are at attention, feet together. Separate the toes so that the feet assume a V position (heels together, toes apart).

Step 2: Separate the heels. You are now standing with feet parallel, about five inches apart.

Step 3: Keep your weight balanced on your toes and bring the heels together in the V position.

Step 4: Bring the toes together. You are now standing at attention.

Step 5: Bend your knees slightly and jump, coming down with your legs apart, knees straight.

Step 6: Jump once more, coming down with both feet together. You are at attention again.

Step 7: Bend the knees slightly and turn the toes toward the right.

Step 8: Turn your heels toward the right and stand at attention.

Hassapikos – 4th Variation.

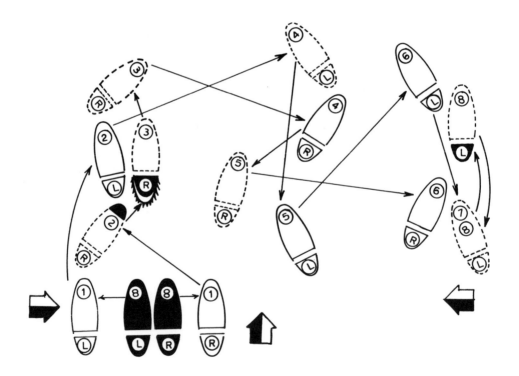

4th Variation – Hassapikos

Jump Steps, Open Steps, Including Basic Steps

Step 1:   Bend your knees slightly and jump, coming down with legs apart, knees straight.

Step 2:   Step forward on the left foot, body leaning forward and both knees bent; simultaneously tap the floor with the right toes close behind the left heel. (The step is identical to basic step 3.)

Step 3:   Brush the right heel alongside the left foot and immediately move the right leg (knee bent) up and down in front of the left leg, without touching the floor. (This step is identical to basic step 4.)

Step 4:   Bring the right foot down behind the left; quickly raise the left leg and kick downward as in step 3. (This step is identical to basic step 5.)

Step 5:   Bring the left foot down behind the right and kick the right leg to the left. (This step is identical to basic step 6.)

Step 6:   Step to the right with the right foot, simultaneously brushing the left foot in front of the right. Both knees should be slightly bent, the weight of the body resting on the left foot. (This step is identical to basic step 7.)

Step 7:   Pull back, shifting the weight of the body to the right foot; simultaneously bring the left foot (toes pointing down and slightly off the floor) in front of the right leg. (This step is identical to basic step 8.)

Step 8:   Quickly touch the floor with the left heel in front of the right foot and immediately return the left foot to its previous position.

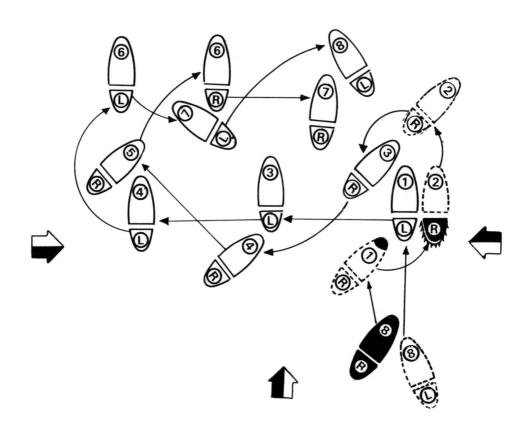

5th Variation – Hassapikos (Grapevine Step)

Three Zigzag Steps to the Left
Three Zigzag Steps to the Right

Step 1: Step forward on the left foot, body leaning forward, both knees bent; simultaneously tap the floor with the right toes close behind the left heel.

Step 2: Brush the right heel alongside the left foot and immediately move the right leg (knee bent) up and down in front of the left leg without touching the floor.

Step 3: Cross the right foot in front of the left. Immediately brush the left foot to the left.

Step 4: Cross the right foot behind the left. Immediately brush the left foot to the left.

Step 5: Cross the right foot in front of the left; all the weight rests on the right leg, knee slightly bent.

Step 6: Bring the left foot forward and cross it in front of the right in a half-circle motion. Immediately brush the right foot to the right.

Step 7: Cross the left foot behind the right. Immediately brush the right foot to the right.

Step 8: Cross the left foot in front of the right; all the weight rests on the left leg, knee slightly bent.

Hassapikos – 6th Variation.

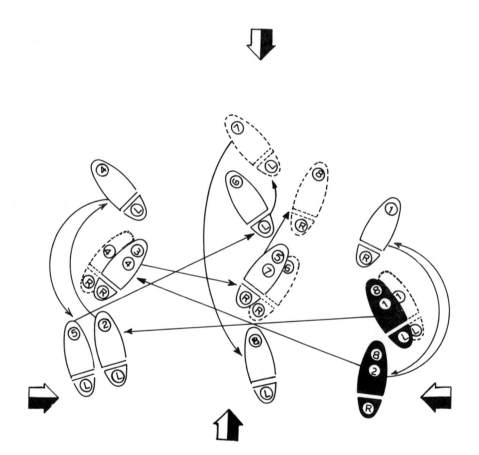

6th Variation – Hassapikos

Zigzag, in Place

Step 1: In a half-circle motion, bring the right foot in front of the left part of the body, leaning forward, both knees bent; quickly raise and lower the left foot. The body is now erect.

Step 2: In a half-circle motion bring the right foot behind the left. Immediately brush the left foot to the left.

Step 3: Cross the right foot in front of the left. All the weight rests on the right leg, knee slightly bent.

Step 4: In a half-circle motion, bring the left foot in front of the right; quickly raise and lower the right foot. The body is now erect.

Step 5: In a half-circle motion bring the left foot behind the right. Immediately brush the right foot to the right.

Step 6: Cross the left foot in front of the right and slightly raise the right foot.

Step 7: Stamp the right foot down in place; simultaneously kick the left leg forward.

Step 8: In a half-circle motion in the air, bring the left leg down behind the right; simultaneously kick the right leg forward.

Hassapikos – 7th Variation.

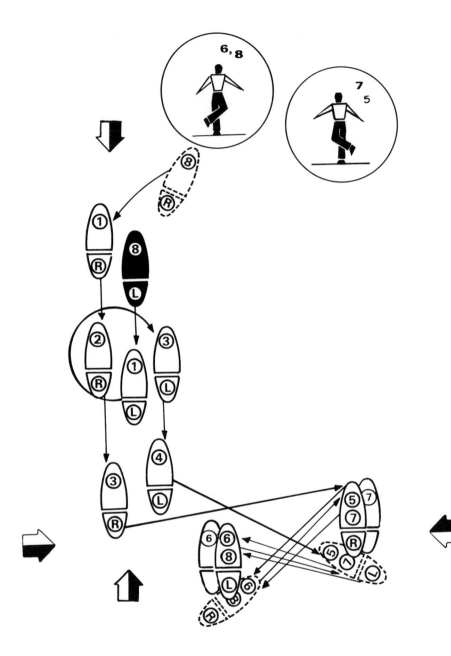

7th Variation – Hassapikos

Hop Steps, Cross, Backward

Step 1: The right leg is in the air. Bring the right leg down, crossing it over the left. (Feet are close together.) Immediately brush the left foot back. (This is a small step.)

Step 2: Brush the right foot back, keeping it crossed in front of the left. (Feet are close together.)

Step 3: In a circular motion bring the left foot behind and around the right foot, crossing the left foot in front of the right. (Feet are close together.) Immediately brush the right foot back.

Step 4: Brush the left foot back, keeping it crossed in front of the right foot. (Feet are close together.)

Step 5: Jump to the right and land on the right foot; simultaneously raise the left leg, knee bent and toes pointing down, behind the right.

Step 6: Jump to the left and land on the left foot; simultaneously raise the right leg, knee bent and toes pointing down, behind the left. Quickly hop in place on the left foot.

Step 7: Jump to the right and land on the right foot; simultaneously raise the left leg, knee bent and toes pointing down, behind the right. Quickly hop in place on the right foot.

Step 8: Jump to the left and land on the left foot; simultaneously raise the right leg, knee bent and toes pointing down, behind the left.

Hassapikos – 8th Variation.

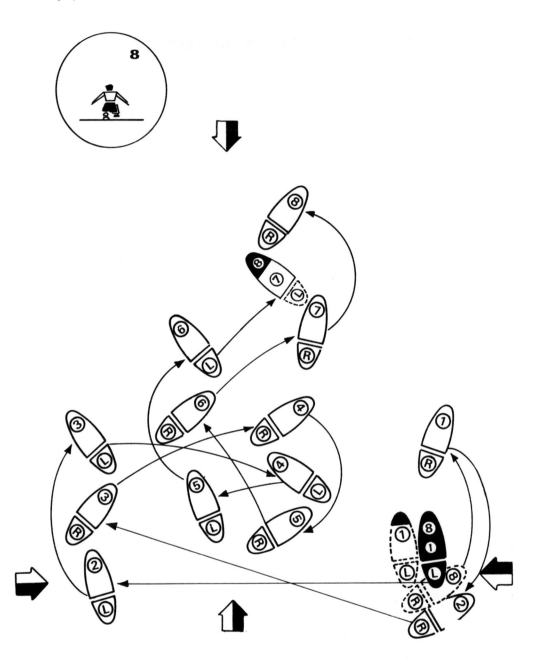

Hassapikos – 8th Variation.

96

8th Variation – Hassapikos

Rounded Cross Steps

Step 1: In a half-circle motion, bring the right foot in front of the left. Both knees are bent, the weight of the body rests on the right leg, and the left foot is on tiptoe.

Step 2: Shifting weight to the left leg, bring the right foot behind the left in a half-circle motion. Immediately brush the left foot to the left.

Step 3: Cross the right foot in front of the left; immediately bring the left foot in front of the right in a half-circle motion.

Step 4: Brush the right foot to the right. Immediately bring the left foot behind the right.

Step 5: Bring the right foot behind the left in a half-circle motion. Immediately brush the left foot to the left.

Step 6: Repeat step 3.

Step 7: Brush the right foot to the right. Immediately bring the left foot in front of the right.

Step 8: Bring the right foot in front of the left and squat. The weight of the body rests on the right leg; the left heel is slightly off the floor.

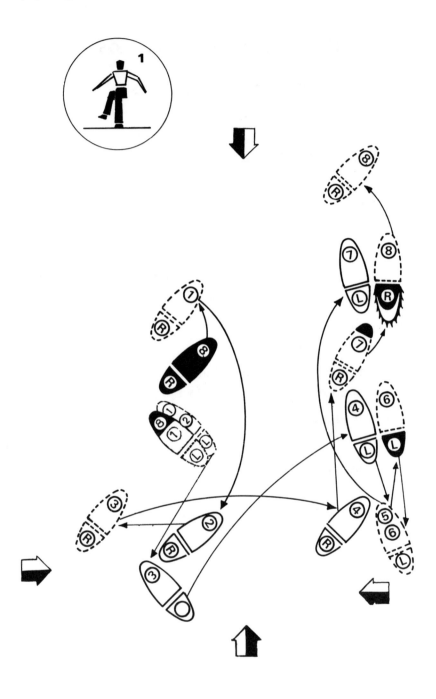

98

9th Variation – Hassapikos

Back Steps

Step 1: Rise from the squatting position, keeping your weight on the right leg. Quickly raise and lower the left foot. Immediately raise the right leg, knee bent, and kick downward.

Step 2: Bring the right foot down behind the left; quickly raise the left leg, kicking downward as in step 1.

Step 3: Bring the left foot down behind the right and kick the right leg to the left.

Step 4: Step to the right with the right foot; simultaneously brush the left foot in front of the right. Both knees should be slightly bent, the weight of the body resting on the left leg.

Step 5: Pull back, shifting the weight of the body to the right leg; simultaneously bring the left foot (toes pointing down and slightly off the floor) in front of the right leg.

Step 6: Quickly touch the floor in front of the right foot with the left heel and immediately return the left foot to its previous position.

Step 7: Step forward on the left foot, body leaning forward and both knees bent. Simultaneously tap the floor with the right toes close behind the left heels.

Step 8: Brush the right heel alongside the left foot. Immediately raise the right leg, knee bent, and kick downward.

Hassapikos – 10th Variation.

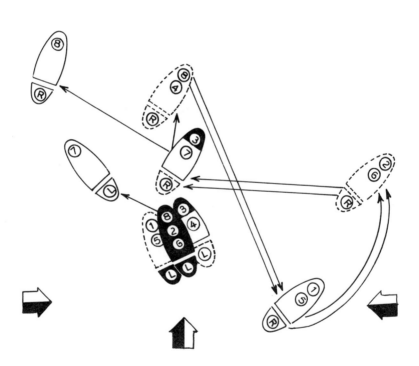

10th Variation – Hassapikos

Squat and Heel Steps

Step 1: Step back and slightly to the right as far as you can with the right foot. Weight rests on the right leg, knee bent. As you tilt backward, straighten the left leg so that only the heel touches the floor.

Step 2: Shift your weight forward to the left leg without bending the knee; simultaneously raise the right leg, knee straight, a few inches off the floor, toward the right.

Step 3: Bring the right foot down in front of the left and squat on the balls of both feet.

Step 4: Rise, shifting your weight to the left leg; simultaneously raise the right leg, knee bent, in front of the left.

Step 5: Repeat step 1.

Step 6: Repeat step 2.

Step 7: Bring the right foot down in front of the left and immediately brush the left foot to the left.

Step 8: Cross the right foot in front of the left as far as possible, bending both knees as you do so. The weight of the body rests on the right leg.

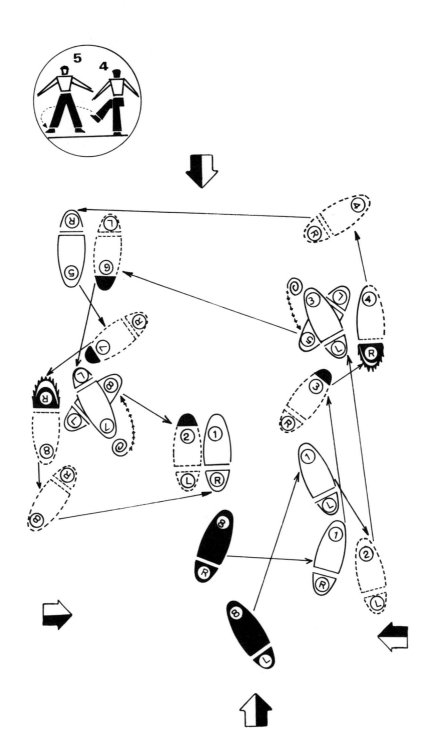

11th Variation – Hassapikos

Turns

Step 1: Shift your weight to the left leg, quickly step to the right with the right foot, and brush the left foot in front of the right. In this position both knees should be slightly bent, the weight of the body resting on the left leg.

Step 2: Pull back, shifting the weight of the body to the right leg; simultaneously bring the left foot (toes pointing down and slightly off the floor) in front of the right leg.

Step 3: Step forward with the left foot, body leaning forward and both knees bent. Simultaneously tap the floor with the right toes close behind the left heel.

Step 4: Brush the right heel alongside the left foot and immediately make a half turn to the left, using the left leg as the pivot and slightly raising the right foot. (You are now facing in the direction opposite to that from which you began.)

Step 5: Step quickly to the right with the right foot.

Step 6: Bring the left foot on tiptoe next to the right.

Step 7: Step forward on the left foot, body leaning forward and both knees bent. Simultaneously tap the floor with the right toes close behind the left heel.

Step 8: Brush the right heel alongside the left foot and immediately make a half turn to the left, using the left leg as the pivot and slightly raising the right foot. (You have now completed one full turn and are facing front again.) If you wish to continue the dance, quickly step to the right with the right foot (step 1). Bring the left foot on tiptoe next to the right foot (step 2). These are the first two steps of the basic hassapikos, and from here you can repeat any or all of the variations.

Hassaposervikos – Basic Steps.

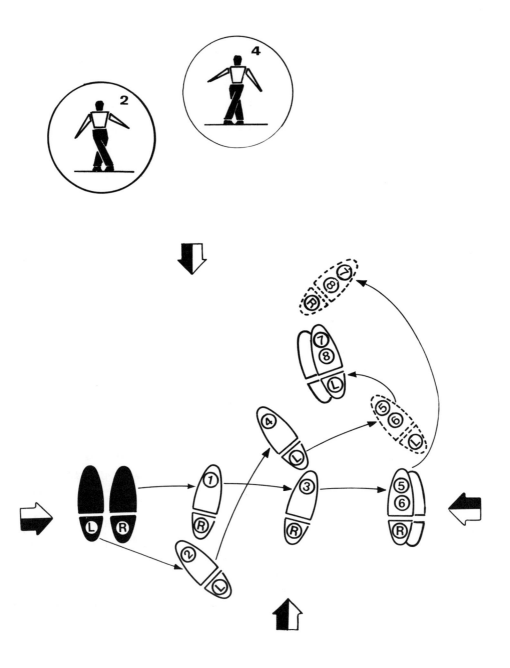

Hassaposervikos

The Hassaposervikos is a continuation of the Hassapikos, in a more intensive and vivid rhythm. Though its history and origin are little known today, it is believed to be a blend of the Hassapikos and a Serbian folk dance.

The initial position of the dancers is one of attention. They stand in a straight line, holding shoulders as in the Hassapikos. When space is limited and there are many dancers, they often form a circle and dance facing inward.

Almost everyone today dances the Hassaposervikos with six steps. This is incorrect because each phrase of the music covers eight steps, the first of which is always danced with the right foot.

Note: All of these dances are very fast. Individual movements follow each other in rapid succession.

Basic Steps: 8

Music: 2/4

Initial Position: Dancers stand at attention; they hold each others' shoulders as in the Hassapikos.

Step 1: Step to the right with the right foot.

Step 2: Cross the left foot behind the right.

Step 3: Step to the right with the right foot.

Step 4: Cross left foot in front of the right.

Step 5: Stamp the right foot to the right, simultaneously raising the left leg, knee bent, in front of the right.

Step 6: Hop in place on the right foot.

Step 7: Stamp the left foot to the left, simultaneously raising the right leg, knee bent, in front of the left.

Step 8: Hop in place on the left foot.

Hassaposervikos – 1st Variation.

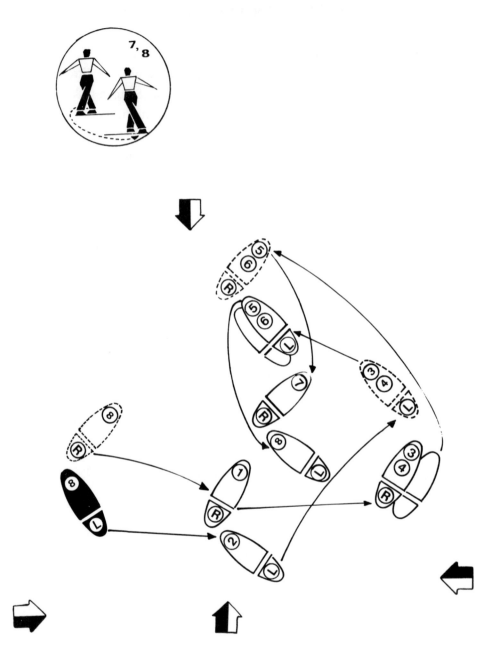

1st Variation – Hassaposervikos

One Cross Step to the Right
Two Cross Steps Back

Step 1:   Step to the right with the right foot.

Step 2:   Cross the left foot behind the right.

Step 3:   Repeat basic step 5.

Step 4:   Repeat basic step 6.

Step 5:   Repeat basic step 7.

Step 6:   Repeat basic step 8.

Step 7:   Quickly hop backward on the left foot, simultaneously bringing the right foot down behind the left foot.

Step 8:   Hop backward on the right foot, simultaneously bringing the left foot down behind the right foot. (Steps 7 and 8 are basically backward skips.)

Hassaposervikos – 2nd Variation.

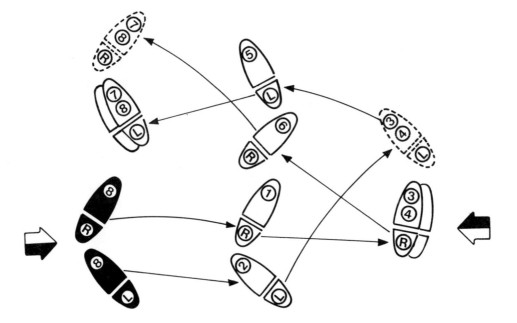

2nd Variation — Hassaposervikos

Four Steps to the Right
Four Steps to the Left

Step 1: Step to the right with the right foot.

Step 2: Cross the left foot behind the right.

Step 3: Stamp the right foot to the right, simultaneously raising the left leg, knee bent, in front of the right.

Step 4: Hop in place on the right foot.

Step 5: Step to the left with the left foot.

Step 6: Cross the right foot behind the left.

Step 7: Stamp the left foot to the left, simultaneously raising the right leg, knee bent, in front of the left.

Step 8: Hop in place on the left foot.

3rd Variation – Hassaposervikos

Right Turns

Step 1: Step to the right with the right foot.

Step 2: Cross the left foot behind the right.

Step 3: (Prepare for a full right turn.) Step to the right with the right foot, turning the body in the same direction as you do so.

Step 4: Using the right leg as the pivot, make a half turn to the right, ending the step with the feet spread apart.

Step 5: Using the left leg as the pivot, make a half turn to the right until you are facing front again. The feet are spread apart.

Step 6: Hop in place on the right foot, simultaneously raising the left leg, knee bent, in front of the right.

Step 7: Repeat basic step 7.

Step 8: Repeat basic step 8.

110

4th Variation – Hassaposervikos

Cross Steps in Place

Step 1: The right foot is raised. Jump to the right and land on the right foot, simultaneously crossing the left foot in front of the right. All your weight is on the left leg; both knees are slightly bent.

Step 2: Quickly raise and lower the right foot. Immediately raise the left leg forward in the air, knee straight.

Step 3: Jump to the left and land on the left foot, simultaneously crossing the right foot in front of the left. All your weight is on the right leg; both knees are slightly bent.

Step 4: Quickly raise and lower the left foot. Immediately raise the right leg forward in the air, knee straight.

Step 5: Repeat basic step 5.

Step 6: Repeat basic step 6.

Step 7: Repeat basic step 7.

Step 8: Repeat basic step 8.

Syrtaki – Basic Steps.

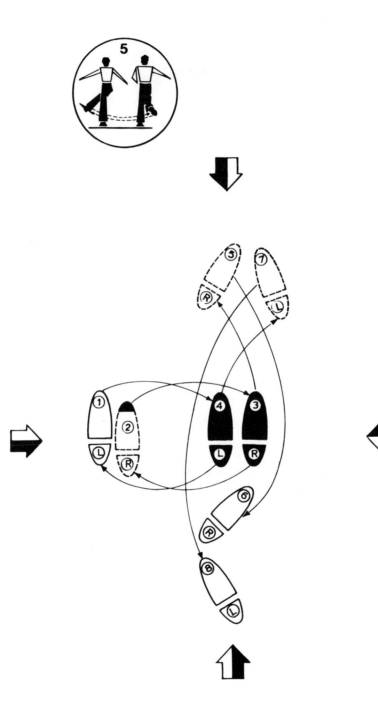

Syrtaki

The Syrtaki, a new dance, is actually a variation of the Hassapikos. The steps are easier than those of the Hassapikos, and perhaps for this reason the Syrtaki is being danced throughout Europe, particularly in France. At the beginning, the Syrtaki is slow, like the Hassapikos; the music then becomes faster, and the dance resembles the Hassaposervikos. The finale of the Syrtaki is the Zorba. (Home orchestras, however, play a consistently slow Syrtaki. This is a matter of preference.)

Most people in the United States confuse the Syrtaki with the Hassapikos. This book will show the differences and the similarities between these two dances.

Remember that each variation begins with the last position of the previous variation.

Basic Steps: 8

Music: 2/4

Initial Position: The Syrtaki is danced in a straight line like the Hassapikos. Dancers stand at attention and place their hands on the shoulders of the dancers on either side.

Step 1: Step to the left with the left foot.

Step 2: Bring the right foot on tiptoe next to the left.

Step 3: Step to the right with the right foot.

Step 4: Stamp the left foot down next to the right.

Step 5: Slightly raise the right leg in place, knee bent and toes pointing down, and immediately kick the right leg to the left.

Step 6: In a half-circle motion, bring the right foot down behind the left.

Step 7: Slightly raise the left leg in place, knee bent and toes pointing down, and immediately kick the left leg to the right.

Step 8: In a half-circle motion, bring the left foot down behind the right.

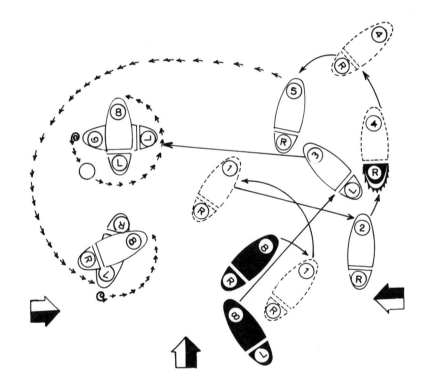

1st Variation — Syrtaki

Step 1: Raise the right leg in place, knee bent and toes pointing down, and immediately kick the right leg to the left.

Step 2: Bring the right foot down, stepping to the right.

Step 3: Cross the left foot in front of the right.

Step 4: Brush the right heel alongside the left foot and immediately kick the right leg forward.

Step 5: Bring the right foot down in front of the left.

Step 6: Step to the left with the left foot as you turn the body to the left. Prepare for a complete left turn.

Step 7: Using the left leg as the pivot, make a half turn to the left in place, bringing the right foot in front of the left.

Step 8: Using the right leg as the pivot, make a half turn to the left in place until you are again facing forward. As you turn, raise the left foot and bring it down in place in front of the right.

Syrtaki – 2nd Variation.

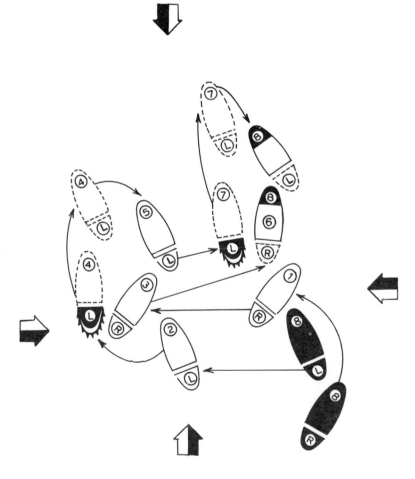

2nd Variation – Syrtaki

Step 1: In a half-circle motion, bring the right foot in front of the left.

Step 2: Brush the left foot to the left.

Step 3: Cross the right foot in front of the left.

Step 4: Brush the left heel alongside the right foot and immediately kick the left leg forward.

Step 5: Bring the left foot down in front of the right.

Step 6: Brush the right foot to the right.

Step 7: Brush the left heel alongside the right foot and immediately kick the left leg forward.

Step 8: Bring the left foot down in front of the right and squat on the balls of both feet.

3rd Variation – Syrtaki

Step 1: Rise from the squatting position; as you do so, raise the right leg in place, knee bent and toes pointing down, and immediately kick the right leg to the left.

Step 2: In half-circle motion, bring the right foot down behind the left.

Step 3: Raise the left leg in place, knee bent and toes pointing down, and immediately kick the left leg to the right.

Step 4: In a half-circle motion, bring the left foot down behind the right.

Step 5: Step to the right with the right foot as you turn the body to the right. Prepare for a complete right turn.

Step 6: Using the right leg as the pivot, make a half turn to the right in place, bringing the left foot in front of the right.

Step 7: Using the left leg as the pivot, make a half turn to the right in place until you are again facing forward. As you turn, raise the right foot and bring it down behind the left.

Step 8: In a half-circle motion, bring the left foot behind the right.

4th Variation — Syrtaki

Step 1:   Brush the right foot to the right.

Step 2:   Bring the left foot on tiptoe next to the right.

Step 3:   Step to the left with the left foot.

Step 4:   Brush the right heel alongside the left foot and immediately kick the right leg forward.

Step 5:   Bring the right foot down in front of the left.

Step 6:   Brush the left heel alongside the right foot and immediately kick the left leg forward.

Step 7:   Bring the left foot down in front of the right.

Step 8:   Jump to the right and land on the right foot; raise the left leg, knee bent and toes pointing down, behind the right.

Note: The variations of the Syrtaki end here, but you may continue dancing by repeating the basic steps and the variations. Begin with your left leg raised behind the right, as in step 8 above. Step to the left with the left foot and continue the basic steps from there.

Syrtaki

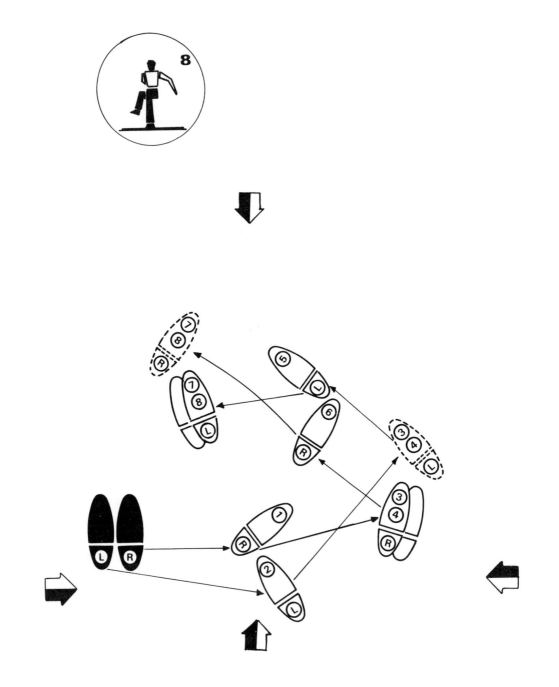

The Zorba

As we mentioned before, the Zorba is the finale of the Syrtaki (which itself is a variation of the Hassaposervikos and the Hassapikos). The Zorba is neither a traditional nor a popular folk dance, having no roots in Greek history. First danced in the well-known movie *Zorba the Greek,* it is a mixture of steps taken from various other Greek dances. Many steps resemble those of the Hassaposervikos, while the fast finale is reminiscent of the Pentozali, a traditional dance of Crete. As a whole, the Zorba is carefree, happy, and spirited, which is why it has become so popular throughout the world—it expresses the Greek temperament in all its moods, joy and pathos, sadness and hope. Remember: To go into the Zorba from the Syrtaki, your right foot must be free.

Steps: 8

Music: 2/4

Initial Position: The dancers stand at attention, in a straight line. They hold each others' shoulders as they do for the Hassapikos. If, however, one wishes to dance this alone, the hands remain free, arms raised.

Basic Steps: Four steps to the right, four steps to the left.

The basic steps are exactly the same as the eight steps of the second variation of the Hassaposervikos (p. 109).

Step 1:   Step to the right foot.

Step 2:   Cross the left foot behind the right.

Step 3:   Stamp the right foot to the right, simultaneously raising the left leg, knee bent, in front of the right.

Step 4:   Hop in place on the right foot.

Step 5:   Step to the left with the left foot.

Step 6:   Cross the right foot behind the left.

Step 7:   Stamp the left foot to the left, simultaneously raising the right leg, knee bent, in front of the left.

Step 8:   Hop in place on the left foot.

Zorba – 1st Variation.

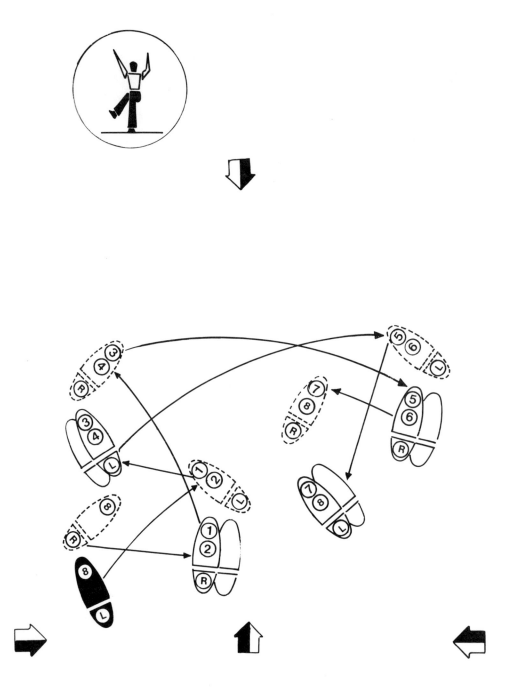

1st Variation – Zorba

Four Steps Forward
Four Steps Backward

In this variation, the dancers' hands are free and raised in the air.

Step 1: Step to the right and slightly forward with the right foot; simultaneously raise the left leg, knee bent, in front of the right.

Step 2: Hop in place on the right foot.

Step 3: Step to the left and slightly forward with the left foot; simultaneously raise the right leg, knee bent, in front of the left.

Step 4: Hop in place on the left foot.

Step 5: Step to the right and slightly backward with the right foot; simultaneously raise the left leg, knee bent, in front of the right.

Step 6: Hop in place on the right foot.

Step 7: Step to the left and slightly backward with the left foot; simultaneously raise the right leg, knee bent, in front of the left.

Step 8: Hop in place on the left foot.

Note: You can double the above variation by dancing eight steps forward and eight steps backward.

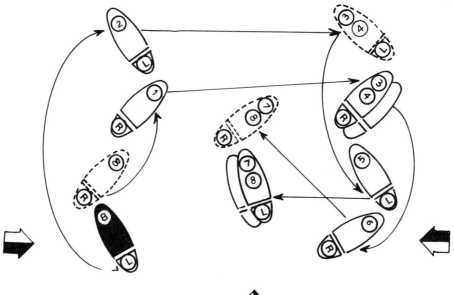

2nd Variation – Zorba

Cross Steps Forward and Backward

Step 1:   Bring the right foot down in front of the left.

Step 2:   In a half-circle motion, bring the left foot in front of the right.

Step 3:   Step to the right with the right foot; simultaneously raise the left leg, knee bent, in front of the right.

Step 4:   Hop in place on the right foot.

Step 5:   In a half-circle motion, bring the left foot down behind the right.

Step 6:   In a half-circle motion, bring the right foot behind the left.

Step 7:   Step to the left with the left foot; simultaneously raise the right leg, knee bent, in front of the left.

Step 8:   Hop in place on the left foot.

3rd Variation – Zorba

Cross Steps Right and Left

Step 1:   Stamp the right foot to the right; simultaneously raise the left leg, knee bent, in front of the right.

Step 2:   Hop in place on the right foot.

Step 3:   Stamp the left foot to the left; simultaneously raise the right leg, knee bent, in front of the left.

Step 4:   Hop in place on the left foot.

Step 5:   Jump to the right and land on the right foot, simultaneously crossing the left foot in front of the right. All your weight is on the left leg; both knees are slightly bent.

Step 6:   Quickly raise the right foot slightly and bring it back down in place; at the same time raise the left leg forward in the air, knee straight.

Step 7:   Jump to the left and land on the left foot, simultaneously crossing the right foot in front of the left. All your weight is on the right leg; both knees are slightly bent.

Step 8:   Quickly raise the left foot slightly and bring it back down in place; at the same time raise the right leg forward in the air, knee straight.

4th Variation – Zorba

In Place

Step 1:   Step forward on the right foot; simultaneously bring the left leg (toes pointing down and knee bent) close behind the right.

Step 2:   Hop in place on the right foot.

Step 3:   Bring the left foot down behind the right; simultaneously raise the right leg, knee bent, in front of the left.

Step 4:   Hop in place on the left foot.

The following four steps are identical to the last four steps of the third variation.

Step 5:   Jump to the right and land on the right foot, simultaneously crossing the left foot in front of the right. All your weight is on the left leg; both knees are slightly bent.

Step 6:   Quickly raise the right foot slightly, and bring it back down in place; at same time raise the left leg forward in the air, knee straight.

Step 7:   Jump to the left and land on the left foot, simultaneously crossing the right foot in front of the left. All your weight is on the right leg; both knees are bent.

Step 8:   Quickly raise the left foot slightly and bring it back down in place; at the same time raise the right leg forward in the air, knee straight.

Note: You may repeat the variations as many times as you wish. The Zorba music is both slow and fast—the first two variations are suited to the slow beat, while the last two variations are better suited to the quick beat. It is important to follow the beat of the music and to begin the dance at the right point.

Zorba

132

The Zorba dance.

The Zeibekikos.

134

Zeibekikos

The Zeibekikos is believed to be the dance of Greeks who immigrated to Asia Minor from Thrace. These immigrants, called *zeibekoi* or *zeibekides* (brave fighters) by the Turks, forsook their Greek Orthodox religion and constituted a separate class of Muslims in the Turkish provinces of Proussis and Aidinious. Historians believe that they were descendants of the ancient Thracians who, throughout the centuries, maintained the character and customs of their ancestors. It is highly probable that the Zeibekikos is an ancient Thracean dance.

The Zeibekikos was originally danced only by men, but today it is also danced by women. It is a very free dance, usually performed by a single dancer or by a couple facing each other. Each dancer can improvise according to his imagination, following the rhythm of the music as best he can.

The Zeibekikos has the beat of 9/8, and often the steps vary according to the song.

Stance in the Zeibekikos

In performing the Zeibekikos, the dancer dances only for himself, as though no one exists around him. His arms droop slightly, the hands are palms down, and the shoulders are thrust slightly forward. His attitude is serious, almost morose, and the steps range from slow and steady to quick— two steps to the beat.

It is important that the student of the Zeibekikos learn the beat of the music well before beginning the lesson. He should listen to the Zeibekikos music over and over again to familiarize himself with it.

Note: If you are to dance in public, begin by making several circle steps around the dance floor until you catch the beat of the music and are ready to begin the basic steps. In some variations of the Zeibekikos, all eight steps are done more or less in place. To make the diagrams more comprehensible, I have spread out the steps on the illustrations. The student must dance these steps while remaining in the same position, as explained in the variations.

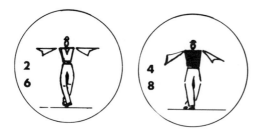

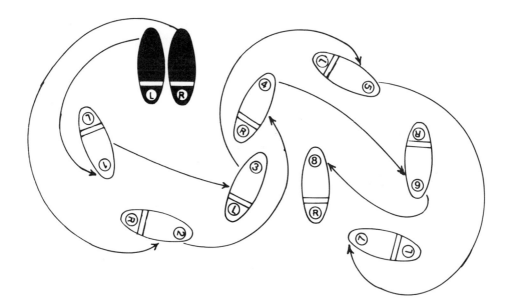

Zeibekikos

Right and Left Turns

Basic Steps: 8

Music: 9/8

In the first four steps, the dancer makes one open (walking) left turn. In the second four steps, the dancer makes one open right turn.

Step 1: Face left and step to the left with the left foot.

Step 2: Using the left leg as the pivot, turn to the left until you are facing in the direction opposite to that from which you began. Bring the right foot in front of the left.

Step 3: Face left and step to the left with the left foot.

Step 4: Using the left leg as the pivot, turn to the left until you are facing front again. Bring the right foot in front of the left.

Step 5: Face right and bring the left foot in a half-circle motion in front of the right.

Step 6: Using the left leg as the pivot, turn to the right until you are facing in the direction opposite to that from which you began. Bring the right foot in front of the left.

Step 7: Face right and bring the left foot in a half-circle motion in front of the right as you turn the body to the right.

Step 8: Using the left leg as the pivot, turn to the right until you are facing front again. Bring the right foot in front of the left.

Zeibekikos — 1st Variation.

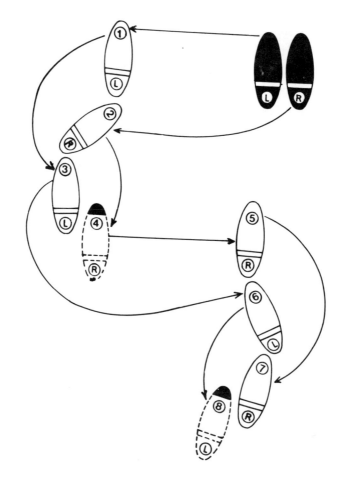

1st Variation – Zeibekikos

Cross Steps Back

Step 1:   Step to the left with the left foot.

Step 2:   Cross the right foot behind the left.

Step 3:   Bring the left foot in a half-circle motion behind the right.

Step 4:   Bring the right foot on tiptoe next to the arch of the left.

Step 5:   Step to the right with the right foot.

Step 6:   Cross the left foot behind the right.

Step 7:   Bring the right foot in a half-circle motion behind the left.

Step 8:   Bring the left foot on tiptoe next to the arch of right.

Zeibekikos – 2nd Variation.

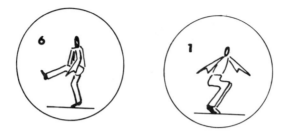

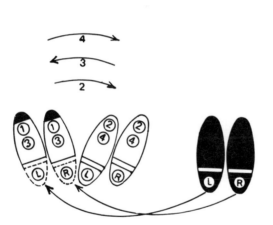

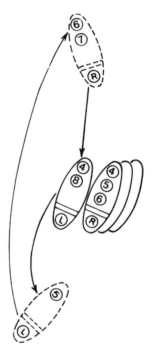

2nd Variation – Zeibekikos

Squat and Jump

Step 1:   Jump to the left and land in a squat on the balls of both feet. (Feet and knees are together.)

Steps 2, 3, and 4:   Maintaining the squat position, knees together, turn both feet to the right, to the left, and to the right again, balancing your weight between the toes and the heels.

Step 5:   Rise and hop on the right foot, in place, simultaneously raising the left leg back, knee straight. (The body leans forward slightly.)

Step 6:   Hop on the right foot again, simultaneously swinging the left leg forward in the air, knee straight; clap hands under the left leg.

Step 7:   Hop on the right foot and tap the left toes with the back of the right hand.

Step 8:   Bring the left foot down next to the right.

Zeibekikos — 3rd Variation.

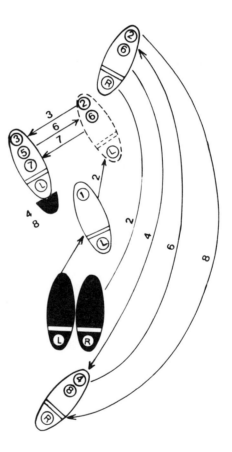

3rd Variation — Zeibekikos

Steps Forward, Backward

Step 1:   Step forward with the left foot.

Step 2:   Bring the right foot in front of the left in a half-circle motion (the right knee is bent, the body leans forward); simultaneously bring the left foot, toes pointing down and slightly off the floor, close behind the right leg.

Step 3:   Bring the left foot down behind the right.

Step 4:   Step back as far as you can with the right foot. Weight rests on the right leg, knee bent. As you tilt backward, straighten the left leg so that only the heel touches the floor.

Step 5:   Shift your weight forward to the left leg, without bending the knees.

Steps 6, 7, and 8:   Repeat steps 2, 3, and 4.

Zeibekikos – 4th Variation.

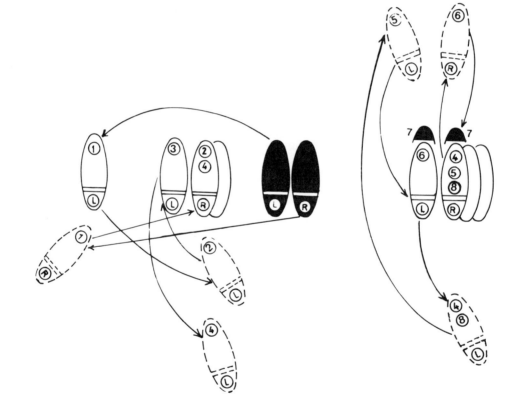

4th Variation — Zeibekikos

Tapped Scissors Step

Step 1:   Jump to the left and land on the left foot, bringing the right foot, toes pointing down and slightly off the floor, close behind the left leg.

Step 2:   Jump to the right and land on the right foot, bringing the left foot, toes pointing down and slightly off the floor, close behind the right leg.

Step 3:   Stamp the left foot next to the right.

Step 4:   Hop in place on the right foot, simultaneously raising the left leg back, knee straight. (The body leans forward slightly.)

Step 5:   Hop on the right foot, simultaneously swinging the left leg, knee straight forward, in the air; tap the left toes with the right hand.

Step 6:   Jump in place, bringing the left leg down and raising the right leg, knees straight, forward in the air as you do so; tap the right toes with the left hand.

Step 7:   Jump in place, bringing the right foot down next to the left and squat on the balls of both feet.

Step 8:   Rise and hop on right foot, simultaneously raising the left leg back, knee straight. (The body leans forward slightly.)

Zeibekikos – 5th Variation.

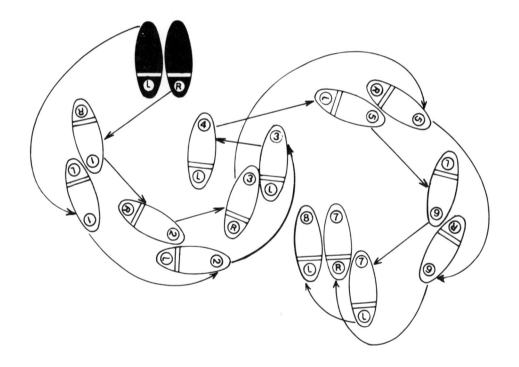

5th Variation — Zeibekikos

Left and Right Turns
Double Steps

Each turn is completed with four circular steps: three double and one single.

Step 1: Face left and step to the left with the left foot; immediately bring the right toes next to the left side of the left heel (the left leg is crossed in front of the right).

Steps 2 and 3: Repeat step 1 twice, turning to the left until you are facing front center again. In this position the left leg is still crossed in front of the right.

Step 4: Uncross legs by stepping to the left with the left foot.

Step 5: Face right and step to the right with the right foot; immediately bring the left toes next to the right side of the right heel (the right leg is crossed in front of the left).

Steps 6 and 7: Repeat step 5 twice, turning to the right until you are facing front center again. In this position, the right leg is still crossed in front of the left.

Step 8: Uncross the legs by bringing the left foot next to the inside of the right.

Zeibekikos – 6th Variation.

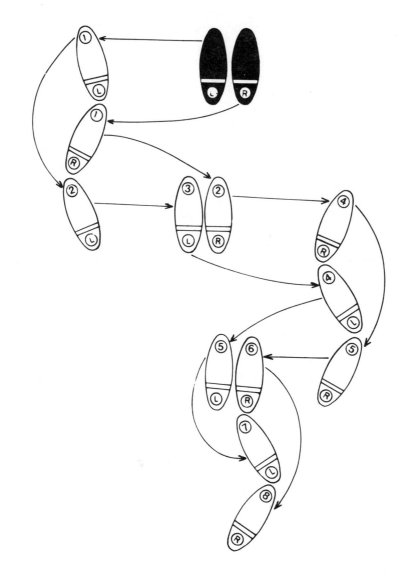

6th Variation — Zeibekikos

Side Brush Steps

Step 1:   Brush the left foot to the left and quickly brush the right foot behind the left.

Step 2:   Brush the left foot behind the right in a half-circle motion; quickly brush the right foot to the right.

Step 3:   Brush the left foot next to the right.

Steps 4, 5, and 6:   Repeat steps 1, 2, and 3 above in the opposite direction by brushing the right foot to the right.

Step 7:   Brush the left foot behind the right in a half-circle motion.

Step 8:   Brush the right foot behind the left in a half-circle motion.

Zeibekikos

San ton ae to i ha fte ra o o o   ke pe ta ga   ke pe ta-

ga po li psi la   ma e na he ri la tre me   no

e na he ti la trefto

151

Popular Folk Music

After the Greek Revolution of 1821 brought liberation to the Greek people, they slowly began to take on the European way of life. As people were drawn to urban areas, business activity was created, bringing new habits and new forms of cultural and intellectual expression.

The popularity of the traditional or demotic song faded as the people who had exchanged the *foustanella* for trousers also took on the music of Europe. And so the new urban song arrived in Greece—the Kantada, a hybrid of Italian and German music.

Soon after World War I, a new dance music—the Tango—conquered the world, and with it Greece. For thirty years, the Tango was the foremost dance music in the country.

Yet the less sophisticated, poorer classes of Greeks still held onto their traditions and found enjoyment in their own style of music—a music that reflected the pessimism and the wounded spirit of their downtrodden lives.

From these people, the people of the underground, as they are known, came the Rebetiko, the popular folk song that slowly evolved into the form we know today.

It seems the people were tired of European music and looked for something else, something they could feel more deeply, something that better expressed their emotions. They found it in the popular folk song.

And so the past twenty years have been the beginning of a new trend, the popular folk song that started out in small urban cafes and quickly won over Greeks of all social classes. This was spurred on by contemporary composers, who gave a new form and impetus to popular folk music, among them Manos Hadjidakis, the famous composer of "Never on Sunday," and Mikis Theodorakis, composer of the Z film score.

Today the popular folk style, the music of the bouzouki, accompanies the modern folk dances and is accepted throughout Greece and wherever Greek communities have taken root.

The Popular Folk Orchestra

The main instrument in the popular folk orchestra is always the bouzouki. It is also the oldest instrument, believed to be related to the *pan-douris* of the ancient Greek. (Some claim that the bouzouki was known to the pre-Hellenic cultures of Egypt, Assyria, China, and India.)

The bouzouki is a string instrument made of wood, with an arm twenty-four to twenty-eight inches long, and three pairs of chords.

In earlier times, the bouzouki came in a number of variations, most of which have been lost. The only one remaining is the baglamas or baby bouzouki, as it is called because of its small size. Over twenty years ago, the popular folk orchestra consisted of three or four bouzoukis, a baglamas, a guitar, a violin, a piano, an accordion, and the *defi*. A characteristic of this orchestra was that the musicians and the singers played and sang while seated. Today the popular folk orchestra has replaced the piano and accordion with the organ, and has added wind instruments and drums. Of course, the bouzouki plays the most important role; on occasion a baglama is included in a modern orchestra.

A modern folk orchestra. The bouzouki player is at the right.

153

Left, Queen Amalia costume. Right, a woman's costume from Attica in central Greece. (Photos courtesy of the Historical Museum of Athens.)

Greek Costumes

Greek costumes have very ancient roots, mostly in the Byzantine period. Although at first sight this may not be obvious, upon careful scrutiny one will see that the clothing of the 1800s has many similarities to the styles of the very early periods.*

Women's Folk Costumes

In contrast to men's costumes, women's clothing maintained the traditional shape and trimmings despite the varied influences of the passing years. This is due to the fact that Greek women traveled rarely, in comparison to men.

Such a wide variety of women's costumes had developed that there were soon three and often more variations of the same dress in every town or province of Greece. (It had been customary for each village to have one style unique to it.) In spite of this large variety we can divide women's costumes into three main categories: costumes of the mountain regions, costumes of the plains, and costumes of the islands. Each of these groups can be further subdivided into urban and rural styles.

It would take volumes to analyze in detail the many variations of Greek costume with its domestically woven cloth, its unique weaving and embroidery work, the numerous trimmings and accessories, the vivid colors, the many and varied head scarfs, the different types of jewelry, etc.

The purpose of the Greek women's costume is not to show off the shape of the body but to cover it decoratively, with pomp and flair. In fact, it is so overbearing that oftentimes the viewer is distracted from the beauty and

* What are now considered Greek costumes as such, were actually the dress of the period. Greek costumes are now worn only at festivals or commemorative occasions.

155

grace of the dance when he notices the intricate embroidery and the trimmings of the dancer's dress.

The richness of Greek costumes was due mainly to the lack of security, and ignorance in money transactions, which resulted in many early Greeks putting their wealth into clothing and jewelry. Obviously a great deal of time and labor goes into the making of every costume.

Once, on the Greek island of Kos, I saw a little old lady sitting on the stoop of her courtyard, embroidering her daughter's wedding dress. I asked her how long she had been working on it, and you can imagine my surprise when she replied that she had been working on it for fourteen months and needed much more time to complete it.

The Undergarments

The shirt (*poukamiso*), which is never omitted in the Greek traditional costume, is made of cotton or silklike linen. It reaches the floor and is usually decorated on the sleeves or the hem, which are the only two parts visible underneath the main dress.

The petticoat (*misofori*), made of muslin, is a skirt worn over the shirt and under the main dress or skirt of certain costumes.

The panties (*vraka*) are made of muslin.

The Outer Garments

The coat-dress (*forema-palto*), a main garment, is usually made of expensive material decorated with multicolored, heavy embroidery. It is worn over the above undergarments.

The skirt (*fousta*), also a main garment, is made of wool or silk. It is always worn with the *sigouni* or *kontogouni* but may or may not be worn with the coat-dress.

The *sigouni*, a jacket without sleeves, made of woven wool and decorated with heavy embroidery. It is worn over the main garment (coat-dress or skirt) when the main garment is of a light material.

The *kontogouni* or *zipouni* is a form of short vest that may or may not be decorated with gold embroidery or multicolored braiding. It is worn over the shirt with the skirt or often over the main dress. The summer version is made of lighter material than the winter one.

Left, dress from the island of Skiros. Right, the traditional costume of Epirus, Greece. (Photos courtesy of the Historical Museum of Athens.)

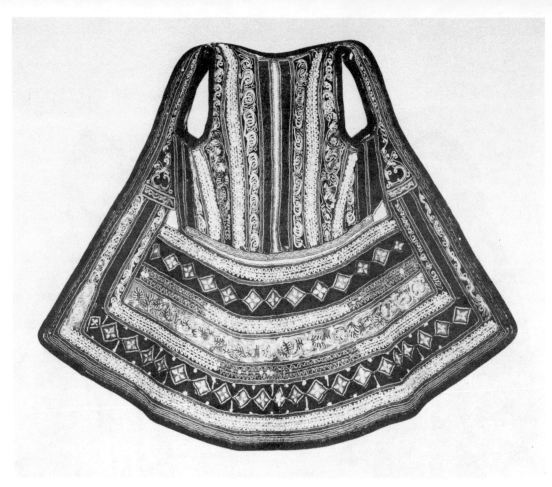

The kontogouni. (Photo courtesy of the Museum of Popular Handcrafts, Athens, Greece.)

Below, woman's gold carved belt buckle. Opposite, the podia (apron). (Photos courtesy of the Folk Museum of Macedonia.)

Accessories

The following accessories are important and necessary complements to the woman's costume:

The apron (*podia*) accompanies most costumes. It is usually made of woven wool, cotton, or silklike linen. It may be completely embroidered or decorated with braiding and lace.

The belt (*zonari*) is very long and wraps many times around the waist. It is usually made of cotton-wool material with multicolored stripes or else is solid-colored. The belt is decorated with buckles or is made of copper or silver. The buckles and the belts are valuable and come in a great variety of designs and shapes. They are some of the most impressive of the costume's accessories.

The adornments worn around the neck consist of many gold or silver chains from which hang gold coins or tiny, multicolored beads.

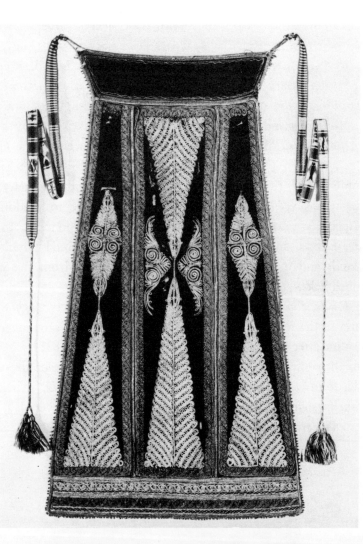

The adornments of the head are varied, the most common being a kerchief tied in many different ways. It is trimmed either with gold coins, tassels, or flowers, according to the dress. The kerchief is made of cotton or silk and can be solid or multicolored.

Men's Folk Costumes

Greek costumes for men are radically different from women's costumes. Free of adornments and varied colors, they retained their basic configuration throughout the centuries.

Men's costumes, like those of the women, are rooted in an ancient tradition. Nevertheless, various historical and social factors in the eighteenth century created some changes and variations in the basic costume.

There are two major categories of male folk dress: costumes of the land and costumes of the sea. Each group also has urban and rural variations.

In earlier times, long dress-coats with wide sleeves (*anteria*) were worn by men in the cities. In the villages, it was customary to wear the *panovraki* (literally, overpants), woolen trousers, either in white or in a dark color, narrow at the bottom and wide at the waist and crotch. With this, the men wore the *poukamiso,* a type of short dress worn either straight in one piece or gathered at the waist and pleated from there to the hips. The color and material of the *poukamiso* differed according to the province and the age of the wearer.

As time passed, the *foustanella,* a pleated skirt made of many yards of white muslin, evolved from the *poukamiso* and came to predominate in Greece, especially in central Greece and in the Peloponnese. In Thrace, Macedonia, Epirus, and elsewhere, the *panovraki* remained popular; while on the islands and in coastal areas, the *vraka,* derived from the *panovraki* and described below, became a staple of regional dress.

The *foustanella* was adopted by the Greek fighters (*armatoloi* and *klefts*) early in the revolutionary period, and King Othon sanctioned it as an official costume after Greece's liberation from the Turks in 1821.

From then on, in the cities where the Western mode of dress did not prevail, the *foustanella* slowly took the place of the *anteria;* in the villages the *foustanella* soon became the formal, and often the everyday, dress of Greek men. The *vraka* continued popular on the islands and in coastal areas.

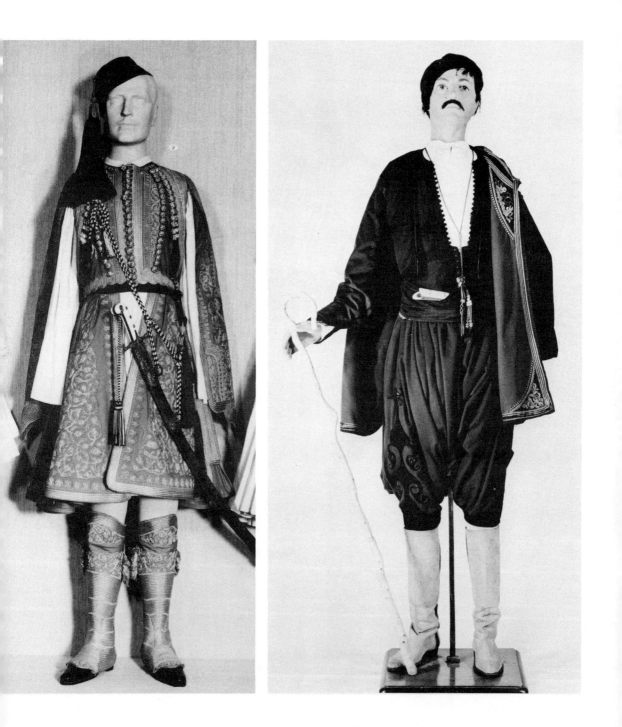

Left, formal foustanella costume worn by Greek Government officials in the nineteenth century. (Photo courtesy of the Benaki Museum, Athens, Greece.) Right, the Cretan vraka. (Photo courtesy of the Historical Museum of Greece.)

The Foustanella.

The Foustanella

The *foustanella* is a form of white skirt with many folds and pleats. A full bolt of material, muslin or linen, is needed for one *foustanella*. In earlier times, the *foustanella* was long, below the knee, but the modern one is very short, above the knee.

The *fermezi* (jacket) is a short vest made of velvet or serge in blue or red, embroidered with gold or other colored piping. The sleeves (*manikia*) were slung over the back.

The waist-high stockings are made of white cotton.

The shirt is usually made of white muslin, linen, or silk, and has very wide sleeves.

Accessories for the Foustanella

The traditional *zonari,* a form of belt, is worn at the waist. The *zonari* is made of wool or cotton fabric in multicolors or of one solid color.

Black garters are worn over the white stockings beneath the knee.

Tsarouhia are worn on the feet. These are shoes made of hard leather with a pointed toe on which sits a large black pompon.

On the head, a cap is worn from which hangs a large tassel on an attached cord.

The Vraka Outfit

The *vraka* is a form of loose, somewhat fluffed-out pants with a long crotch, particularly so from the rear. It is made of serge, wool, or cotton.

There are many variations of the *vraka,* but the one from Crete is considered outstanding in cut and design.

The color of the Cretan *vraka* is usually dark blue, while those of the other islands are white or black.

A vest with single or double buttonholes and usually without sleeves is worn over the shirt. The vest is embroidered with cord around the neck and at the buttonholes. The material and the color are the same as that of the *vraka.*

Complementing the vest of the Cretan costume is the cape (*kapota*), adorned with multicolored embroidery and a red lining.

The panovraki worn by a man from northern Greece.

Accessories for the Vraka

The *zonari,* a very wide and extremely long belt (about nine yards), is always of a solid color.

The kerchief worn by the men of Crete has fringe that hangs over the brow. In the other islands the men wear caps.

White or black boots usually complete the costume. Otherwise multicolored knee-length stockings may be worn with regular shoes.

These Greek male costumes are seen today only in certain remote villages of Greece where the old men have refused to modernize their dress. In addition, various dancing groups performing at ethnic events carry on the traditional folk dress.

Dance of Cephalonia. Demoglou Dancers wearing the vraka.

Evzones dancing in the foustanella costume.

The Evzones

In the center of Athens, near the presidential mansion, is a special unit of Greek soldiers who wear the full traditional *foustanella* costume. They were formerly the royal palace guards chosen for their height, weight, and well-developed physique. Today they guard the President of Greece and the Tomb of the Unknown Soldier on Constitution Square.

Let's Have a Greek Party

And now, my friends, that you have learned some of the entertaining Greek dances, surprise your friends with an invitation to your home for a special night of Greek music and dancing, Greek food and drink.

To give a Greek atmosphere to the evening, decorate your rooms with huge, colorful posters of Greece; you can obtain such posters from the Hellenic Tourist Organization on Fifth Avenue in New York. Hang up a Greek flag and a *tsarouhi* (the Greek shoe worn by the Evzones).

What should you wear? Since it's quite difficult to obtain original Greek costumes, you can add some Greek trimmings to your own clothes. Or you may visit various Greek boutiques such as Greek Island Ltd. in New York City, where you can pick up beautiful Greek peasant shirts, skirts, and blouses.

The hostess can wear a solid-color skirt, short or long, and a white blouse with wide sleeves. You can buy or make an apron and a vest and trim them with colored borders. Or wear a colored sash around your waist and gold coins around your neck. You might even wear a head scarf like the peasant women.

The host can wear a pair of black pants, white shirt, and a red sash around his waist. Those who sew can make a man's shirt with full pleated sleeves that hang very wide at the cuffs. Or simply wear an ordinary long-sleeved white shirt and fold back the cuffs. A vest, like the women's, is also attractive.

Now for the music. There is an ample supply of Greek records in the Greek shops of your city; some Greek records may be found in regular record and department stores. Your stereo will bring you the sound of a full Greek bouzouki orchestra. If you want to be really lavish, you might hire a two- or three-piece band. Such groups frequently advertise in the Greek-American newspapers throughout the United States.

Dance of Cephalonia (Demoglou Dancers).

Now for food and drink. As an aperitif you must, of course, serve *ouzo*. Serve it with hors d'oeuvres such as *taramosalata* (fish roe dip), tiny meatballs (*keftedakia*), stuffed grape leaves (*dolmadakia*), and small cheese triangles (*tiropites*). Your main course should consist of either one or all of the following: *moussaka* (eggplant casserole), *pastitsio* (the macaroni-béchamel sauce wonder), *souvlaki* (shish kebab), and a Greek salad of tossed greens, tomatoes, black olives, and feta cheese. The wine will be Retsina, or for those who cannot get used to the resin taste of this popular Greek wine, a rosé, preferably Roditys, or a white Demestica. For dessert serve *baklava* or *galaktoboureko* (creamy custard wrapped in thin pastry covered with syrup). You can order these from various Greek restaurants, catering shops, and/or bakeries. You might even have a Greek friend help you make them yourself. *The Art of Greek Cookery* (Garden City, N.Y.: Doubleday & Company, Inc.) contains recipes for all these foods and dozens of others just as mouthwatering.

I bid you yiassou and good luck in your dancing.

And so I have given you all the ingredients for a festive Greek party or for a simple evening of fun and dancing with a few friends. Remember all that I have told you. Relax and enjoy! Eat, drink, and be merry the happy Greek way, with the dances you have learned here.

Now that I have come to the end of my book, my friends, I feel a sense of joy and of sadness. Joy for all I have shared with you, and sadness that I could not give you more. I want to believe that in that vast garden of the dance, I was able to pick a small bouquet of lovely flowers and hand them to you. I hope you learn to love this little volume and give it a chance to accompany you in many pleasant moments of your life as you dance the spirited dances of Greece.

Good luck . . . and *yiassou!*

Rozanna

Index

Accessories:
    men's, 163
    women's, 155, 158
        (illustration), 159
Accordion, 153
Acoustics, Pythagorean
        theory of, 73
Akritans, 73
Amalia costume, Queen, 154
        (illustration)
Amané, 73
Anastenaria (fire-walking
        dance), 12–13
    illustrations, 14, 15, 170
Ancient dances, 1–3
Anteria (dress-coats), 160
Appetizers:
    dolmadakia, 169
    keftedakia, 169
    taramosalata, 169
    tiropites, 169
Apron (podia), 158
        (illustration), 159
Arcadian dances, 8
Armatoloi (warriors), 160
Art of Greek Cookery, The,
        169
Athena (goddess), 2
Athena (Archaeological
        Museum, Athens),
        xvi
Attica, women's costumes of,
        154 (illustration)

Baglamas (musical
        instrument), 153
Baklava, 169
Baresci, Joseph, xiii
Belts:
    buckles, 158 (illustration),
        159
    men's, 163
    women's, 159
Bouzouki (musical
        instrument), 153
Bouzouki music, 16, 152
    instrument, 153
    live, 168
    records, 168
Brush cross step, Syrtos, 45
Buckles, women's shoe, 158
        (illustration), 159
Byzantine liturgical music,
        73

Cape (kapota), 163
Caps, 163
Cephalonia, dance of, 169
Cheese:
    feta, 169
    tiropites (triangles), 169
Circular dances, 40
Clarinet, 72 (illustration)
Classic period, Greek, 1
Coastal area men's costumes,
        160
Coat-dress:
    man's (anteria), 160
    woman's (forema-palto),
        156
Constantine, St., 12–13
Constantinople, fall of, 73
Corfu wedding dance, 18
        (illustration)
Costumes:
    accessories:
        men's, 163
        women's, 159
    anteria (man's dress-coat),
        160
    Byzantine origin, 155
    Epirus, 157 (illustration)
    fabrics, 155
    fermezi (man's jacket),
        163
    forema-palto (woman's
        coat-dress), 156
    fousta (woman's skirt),
        156
    foustanella, 17, 162
        (illustration)
        abandonment, 152
        evolution, 160
        Evzones' use of, 166
        (illustration), 167
        as official wear, 161
        (illustration)
    kapota (cape), 163
    kontogouni (woman's
        vest), 156
    manikia (man's sleeves),
        163
    men's, 160–67
        accessories, 163
        foustanella, 17, 152, 160,
        167
        illustrations, 161, 162,
        166
        improvised, 168

    official, 160, 161
        (illustration)
    popular dances, for, 17
    variety, 160
    misofori (woman's
        petticoat), 156
    origins, 155
    panovraki (man's
        trousers), 160, 163,
        164 (illustration)
    podia (apron), 158
        (illustration), 159
    popular dances, for, 17
    poukamiso (shirt)
        man's, 160
        woman's, 156
    rural, 155, 160
    sigouni (woman's
        sleeveless jacket), 156
    Skiros, of, 157
        (illustration)
    trimming:
        men's, 163
        women's, 155, 156
    tsarouhia (boots), 163
    urban, 155, 160
    vraka (man's trousers),
        160, 161
        (illustration), 163
    vraka (woman's panties),
        156
    women's, 155–56
        accessories, 159
        Attic, 154 (illustration)
        Epirus, of, 157
        fabrics, 155
        improvised, 168
        popular dances, for, 17
        Queen Amalia, 154
        (illustration)
        Skiros, of, 157
        (illustration)
        traditional dances, for,
        17
        trimming, 155, 156
        variety, 155
    zipouni (woman's vest)
        156
    zonari (belt):
        man's, 163
        woman's, 159
Couple dances, 135
Crete:
    dances, 1, 2, 5, 8

lyres carved in, 74
men's costumes, 163, 165
Sousta (dance), 5
Cross steps:
  backward, 95
  Hassapikos, 83, 85, 95, 97
  Hassaposervikos, 107, 111
  Kalamatianos, 35
  Syrtos, 49, 51
  Zeibekikos, 139
  Zorba, 127, 128

Dance:
  costume, see Costumes
  defined, 1
  history, 1, 5
  philosophy of, 1–2
  purposes, 1, 2, 3, 5
Dances:
  Anastenaria (fire-walking
    dance), 12–13
    illustrations, 14, 15, 170
  ancient, 1–3
  Arcadian, 8
  Cephalonian, 169
  classification, 2, 16
  couple, 135
  Cretan, 1, 2, 4
    (illustration), 8, 123
  diagrams, explanation of,
    20–21
  Dionysian, 3
  Epirus, of, 8, 9
  fisherman's, 76
    (illustration)
  funeral, 5
  Hassapikos, xi, 16, 78, 79
    (illustration)
    basic steps, 80
      (illustration), 81
    illustrations, 82, 84, 86,
      88, 90, 92, 94, 96, 98,
      100, 102
    Syrtaki as variation, 112
    variations, 79–103, 112
  Hassaposervikos, 16
    basic steps, 104
      (illustration), 105
    Hassapikos and, 105
    illustrations, 106, 108
    origin, 105
    rhythm, 105
    variations, 107–11
  history, 1
  Issos, see subhead: Syrtos
  Kalamatianos, 5, 16, 23,
    26–27 (illustration)
    basic steps, 24
      (illustration), 25
    illustrations, 28, 30, 32,
      34, 36
    variations, 26–37
  Labyrinth dance, 10
    (illustration)
  local, 8

Macedonian, 17
  (illustration), 18
  (illustration)
Masquerade dance, 10
  (illustration)
Pentozali, 4 (illustration),
  123
Pondiak, 11 (illustration)
posture of dancers, 20, 135
Pyrrhic war dance, 2
religious, 2, 3, 12–13
  illustrations, 14, 15, 170
Roumeliotes, of, 8
Salamina, of, 9
  (illustration)
Salonika, of, 18
  (illustration)
social, 5
solo, 135
Sousta, 5
Syrtaki:
  basic steps, 112
    (illustration), 113
  Hassapikos variation, as,
    16, 113, 123
  illustrations, 114, 116
  variations, 115–19
  Zorba as finale, 113, 123
Syrtos, 5, 16
  basic steps, 42
    (illustration), 43
  circular dances, as
    common term for, 40
  illustrations, 44, 46, 48,
    50
  rhythm, 40
  variations, 45–51
Thessaly, of, 8
Thrace, of, 12–13, 135
  illustrations, 14, 15, 170
traditional, 16
Tsakonic, 11 (illustration)
Tsamikos, 16, 54
  (illustration), 55
  illustrations, 60, 62, 64,
    66, 68
  sixteen-step version, 58
    (illustration), 59
  twelve-step version, 56
    (illustration), 57
  variations, 61–69
war dances, 2
wedding dance, 18
  (illustration)
Zalonga, of, 9
Zeibekikos, 16, 134
  (illustration)
  basic steps, 136
    (illustration), 137
  history, 135
  illustrations, 138, 140,
    142, 144, 146, 148
  posture of dancers, 135
  rhythm, 135
  variations, 139–49

Zorba, 16, 132
  (illustration)
  basic steps, 122
    (illustration), 123
  illustrations, 124, 126
  Syrtaki finale, as, 123
  variations, 125–29
Daouli (drum), 75
Dassin, Jules, xiv
  (illustration)
Defi (tambourine), 75, 153
Demestica (wine), 169
Diagrams of dances,
  explanation of, 20–21
Dionysian dances, 3
Dionysos (god), 3
Dolmadakia (stuffed grape
  leaves), 169
Dress-coat:
  man's (anteria), 160
  woman's (forema-palto),
    156
Drinks, Greek, 169
Drums, 75, 153
Dutch Dance Group, xiii

Easter festival, Greece, 6–7
  (illustration)
Eggplant casserole
  (moussaka), 169
Embroidery, 155, 156
Epirus:
  costumes, 157
    (illustration), 160
  dances of, 8, 9
European influence on
  Greek music, 152
Evzones, 167
  illustrations, 70, 166

Fermezi (jacket), 163
Feta cheese, 169
Fire-walking dance
  (Anastenaria), 12–13
  illustrations, 14, 15, 170
Fisherman's dance, 76
  (illustration)
Flag of Greece, 168
Flogera (flute), 75
Flutes, 73 (illustration), 75
Folk dances, popular, 77
Folk music, 73, 152
Food, Greek, 169
Forema-palto (woman's
  coat-dress), 156
Fousta (skirt), 156
Foustanella, 17, 162
  (illustration)
  abandonment, 152
  evolution, 160
  Evzones' use of, 166
    (illustration), 167
  as official wear, 160, 161
    (illustration)
Funerals, dancing at, 5

Galaktoboureko (dessert),
169
Garters, 163
Gounaris, Nicos, xiii
Grape leaves, stuffed
(dolmadakia), 169
Grapevine step, 91
Greek Dance Company,
formation of, xiv
Greek Island Ltd., 168
Greek Islands, costumes of,
160
Greek parties:
costumes:
authentic, 168
improvised, 168
decorations, 168
drinks, 169
food, 169
music, 168
Guitar, 74, 153

Hadjidakis, Manos, 152
Handkerchief use in dances,
18 (illustration), 19
Hassapikos, xi, 16, 78, 79
(illustration)
basic steps, 80
(illustration), 81
Syrtaki as variation, 112
variations:
first, 82 (illustration),
83
second, 84
(illustration), 85
third, 86 (illustration),
87
fourth, 88 (illustration),
89
fifth, 90 (illustration),
91
sixth, 92 (illustration),
93
seventh, 94
(illustration), 95
eighth, 96 (illustration),
97
ninth, 98 (illustration),
99
tenth, 100 (illustration),
101
eleventh, 102
(illustration), 103
Hassaposervikos, 16
basic steps, 104
(illustration), 105
Hassapikos and, 105
origin, 105
rhythm, 105
variations:
first, 106 (illustration),
107
second, 108
(illustration), 109
third, 110

fourth, 111
Head scarves, 155, 160
Helen, Saint, 12–13
icon, 14 (illustration)
Hellenic Tourist
Organization, 168
Homer, dancing mentioned
in, 1

Icons (St. Helen), 14
(illustration)
Improvisation:
costumes for party, 168
dance steps, 22, 23
Issos, see Syrtos

Jackets:
man's (fermezi), 163
woman's (sigouni), 156
Jewelry, 155, 156, 159

Kalamatianos, 5, 16, 23,
26–27 (illustration)
basic steps, 24
(illustration), 25
variations:
first, 26
second, 27
third, 28 (illustration),
29
fourth, 30 (illustration),
31
fifth, 32 (illustration),
33
sixth, 34 (illustration),
35
seventh, 36
(illustration), 37
Kapadokias (Cappadocia),
73
Kapota (cape), 163
Karamouza (flute), 75
Keftedakia (meatballs), 169
Kerchiefs:
man's, 165
woman's, 155, 160
Kleftikos, see Tsamikos
Klefts (warriors), 160
Kontogouni (vest), 156, 158
(illustration)
Kos embroidery, 156
Kourites, 2
Koutsavakides, 16
Krios-Thrace dance, 8
(illustration)

Labyrinth dance, 10
(illustration)
Laouto (guitar), 72
(illustration), 74
Lawson, T. K., 5
Leader, role of, 77
improvisation by, 22, 23
Learning procedure, 20, 22,
77

Leonidas, 2
Licion Hellinidon Dance
Group of Greece, 54
(illustration)
Liturgical music, 73
Local dances, 8
Lyre, 74

Macaroni dish (pastitsio),
169
Macedonia:
costumes, 160
dances of, illustrations, 17,
18
Main dishes, Greek, 169
Manges, 16
Manikia (sleeves), 163
Masquerade dance, 10
(illustration)
Meatballs (keftedakia), 169
Men's costumes:
accessories, 163
foustanella, 17, 162
(illustration)
abandonment, 152
evolution, 160
Evzones' use of, 166
(illustration), 167
as official wear, 161
(illustration)
improvised, 168
official, 160, 161
(illustration)
popular dances, for, 17
variety, 160
Mercouri, Melina, xiv
(illustration)
Misofori (petticoat), 156
Moussaka (eggplant
casserole), 169
Mouzaki, Rozanna:
autobiography, x–xv
dance company, xii, xiii,
xiv
photographs, viii, xi, xiv
Music:
bouzouki, 16, 152, 153, 168
demotic, 73
folk, 73
Kantada, 152
liturgical, 73
orchestral, 72
(illustration), 74–75,
153
Rebetiko, 152
Tango, 152
theory of, 73
traditional, 73
Mycenaeans, 1

Newspapers,
Greek-American, 168
Number of dancers in
group, 77

Orchestras, 72 (illustration),
 74–75, 153
Organ, 153
Othon, King, 160
Ottoman Empire, see Turks
Oud (guitar), 74
Ouzo (drink), 169

Panagyri, 5
Pandouris (musical
 instrument), 153
Panegyris (festival), 5
Panovraki (overpants), 160,
 163, 164 (illustration)
Panties (vraka), 156
Pastitsio (macaroni dish),
 169
Patras, x
Peloponnese, men's costumes
 of, 160
Pentozali (Cretan dance), 4
 (illustration), 123
Percussion instruments, 75
Petticoat (misofori), 156
Phaeakes, 1
Piano, 153
Plato, 2
Podia (apron), 158
 (illustration), 159
Pondiak dance, 11
 (illustration)
Pontos, 73
Posters, 168
Posture of dancers, 20, 135
Poukamiso (shirt)
 man's, 160
 woman's, 156
Pyrrhic war dance, 2
Pythagoras, 73

Queen Amalia costume, 154
 (illustration)

Rea (goddess), 2
Rebetikos, 152
Religious dances, 2, 3
 Anastenaria, 12–13
 illustrations, 14, 15
Retsina (wine), 169
Rockefeller, Nelson, xv
 (illustration)
Roditys (wine), 169
Roumeliotes, dance of, 8
Rozanna Mouzaki Dancers,
 xii, xiii, xiv

Saint Constantine, 12–13
Saint Helen, 12–13
 icon, 14 (illustration)
Salad, Greek, 169
Salamina, dance of, 9
 (illustration)
Salonika, dance of, 18
 (illustration)
Santouri (musical

instrument), 72
 (illustrated), 74
Scarves, 155, 160
Scissors steps:
 Kalamatianos, 37
 Tsamikos, 69
 Zeibekikos, 145
Semele (goddess), 3
Shirt (poukamiso):
 man's, 163
 woman's, 156
Shish kebab, 169
Shoes, men's, 163, 165
Sigouni (sleeveless jacket),
 156
Skiros, costumes of, 157
 (illustration)
Skirt (fousta), 156
Slide steps, 63
Social dances, 5
Sohos, 18 (illustration)
Solo dances, 135
Songs, 73
Sousta (Cretan dance), 5
Souvlaki, 169
Spartans, 2
Spiropoulos, Stavros, x
Squat steps:
 Hassapikos, 101
 Kalamatianos, 33
 Tsamikos, 65
 Zeibekikos, 141
Steps:
 brush cross, 45
 cross:
  backward, 95
  Hassapikos, 83, 85, 95,
   97
  Hassaposervikos, 107,
   111
  Kalamatianos, 35
  Syrtos, 49, 51
  Zeibekikos, 139
  Zorba, 127, 128
 grapevine, 91
 individual dances, see
  Dances; name of
  dance
 scissors step:
  Kalamatianos, 37
  Tsamikos, 69
  Zeibekikos, 145
 slide, 63
 squat:
  Hassapikos, 101
  Kalamatianos, 33
  Tsamikos, 65
  Zeibekikos, 141
Stockings, man's, 163, 165
Stringed instruments, 75
Stuffed grape leaves
 (dolmadakia), 169
Syrtaki:
 basic steps, 112
 (illustration), 113

Hassapikos variation, as,
 16, 113, 123
 variations:
  first, 114 (illustration),
   115
  second, 116
   (illustration), 117
  third, 118
  fourth, 119
 Zorba as finale, 113, 123
Syrtos, 5, 16, 40
 basic steps, 42
  (illustration), 43
 variations:
  first, 44 (illustration),
   45
  second, 46
   (illustration), 47
  third, 48 (illustration),
   49
  fourth, 50 (illustration),
   51

Tambourine (defi), 75
Tango, 152
Taramosalata (fish roe dip),
 169
Terpsichore (muse), 2
Theatrical dances, 5
Theodorakis, Mikis, 152
Thermopylae, 2
Thessalian dances, 8
Thrace:
 costumes, 160
 dances, 12–13, 135
 illustrations, 14, 15
Tiropites (cheese triangles),
 169
Toumbaneli (drum), 75
Trojans, 1
Trousers (panovraki), 160
Tsakonic dance, 10
 (illustration)
Tsamikos, 16, 54
 (illustration), 55
 sixteen-step version, 58
  (illustration), 59
 twelve-step version, 56
  (illustration), 57
 variations:
  first, 60 (illustration),
   61
  second, 62
   (illustration), 63
  third, 64 (illustration),
   65
  fourth, 66 (illustration),
   67
  fifth, 68 (illustration),
   69
Tsarouhia (boots), 163
Turks, 9, 73, 135, 160

Undergarments, women's,
 156

Vests:
    men's, 163
    women's (kontogouni or
        zipouni), 156, 158
        (illustration)
Violin, 72 (illustration), 153
Vraka (man's trousers), 160,
    161 (illustration), 163
Vraka (woman's panties),
    156

War dances, 2
Wedding dances, 18
    (illustration)
Wind instruments, 153
Women:
    costumes, 155–56
        accessories, 159
        Attic, 158 (illustration),
            159
        Epirus, 157
            (illustration)
        fabrics, 155
        improvised, 168
        popular dances, for, 17

Queen Amalia, 154
    (illustration)
Skiros, of, 157
    (illustration)
traditional dances, 17
trimming, 155, 156
variety, 155
and Dance of Zalonga, 9

Zalonga, Dance of, 9
Zeibekikos, 16, 134
    (illustration), 135
    basic steps, 136
        (illustration), 137
    posture of dancers, 135
    rhythm, 135
    variations:
        first, 138 (illustration),
            139
        second, 140
            (illustration), 141
        third, 142 (illustration),
            143
        fourth, 144
            (illustration), 145

fifth, 146 (illustration),
    147
sixth, 148 (illustration),
    149
Zeus (god), 3
Zipouni (vest), 156
Zonari (belts):
    men's, 163, 165
    women's, 159
Zorba, 16, 123, 132
    (illustration)
    basic steps, 122
        (illustration), 123
    variations:
        first, 124 (illustration),
            125
        second, 126
            (illustration), 127
        third, 128
        fourth, 129
Zorba the Greek, dancing
    in, 16, 123
Zouradi School of Ballet, x